Dessertable II
aka
Just Desserts and Deathly Advice

A Collection of
Delectable Desserts
and Tongue-in-Cheek Advice
for the Would-be Murderer

No Crime Unpublished©

Diane Jay Bouchard

Edited by Diane Jay Bouchard
and Gay Toltl Kinman

Legal Notice and Disclaimer
Although every effort has been made to ensure correctness, the recipes in this book may contain errors and omissions. Specific poison dosage information has been deliberately omitted. All material contained in this book is for entertainment purposes only.

The editors and contributors accept no liability for any errors or omissions in this book or for any injuries or losses incurred or resulting from use of the information and recipes in this book.

SinC/LA logo design by Gayle McGary Partlow, Altadena, CA.
Cover by Type Characters, Denver, CO.
Layout and design, 2nd Edition, *Desserticide* aka *Just Desserts and Deathly Advice* by Write Way Publishing, Inc., Aurora, CO email: staff@writewaypub.com

ISBN 0-9679037-0-X
1 2 3 4 5 6 7 8 9 10

Acknowledgements

We wish to thank the Sister in Crime/LA members who so graciously submitted recipes.

A deep appreciation to the award-winning author, Jan Burke, for her delicious introduction, and to Barry A.J. Fisher, Director of the Scientific Services Bureau, Los Angeles County Sheriff's Department, for his contributions.

We wish to express our gratitude to the following crime fighters for generously sharing their expertise: an anonymous homicide detective of Southern California; C.M. Bowers, DDS., Forensic Odontologist; Vickie L. Clawson, Senior Criminalist LASD; Ricki de Kramer, Board of Culinary Historians of Southern California; Beverly A. Kerr, Senior Criminalist LASD; Gisele La Vigne, Senior Criminalist LASD; Susan L. Perez, Criminalist Technician LASD; Anne Riffenburgh, Medical Social Worker; David Sweet, DMD, Ph.D., Director/Bureau of Legal Dentistry, University of British Columbia; and Barbara L. Torres, Senior Criminalist LASD.

A special thank you to Claire Carmichael McNab, author of the Carol Ashton mystery series, children's novels, short stories and articles; instructor UCLA Extension Writer's Program and, since 1997, SinC/National Board member.

This project could not have been done without the help of Donald R. Bouchard; Eric F. Schulte, computer whiz; and Dorrie O'Brien, Write Way Publishing, Inc.

Without everyone's enthusiasm *Desserticide II* would have been nothing more than a great idea.

About Sisters in Crime

Sisters in Crime began in 1986 at the Baltimore Bouchercon when a number of women who read, write, buy, or sell mysteries met for an impromptu breakfast to discuss their mutual concerns. At a minimum, they hoped to develop camaraderie and to learn what women in the mystery field really wanted. There was a perception that women writers were reviewed less frequently and that their books were taken less seriously than those written by men.

Sara Paretsky was the driving force in galvanizing and organizing the group. In May of 1987, the first steering committee was elected.

In 1989, in keeping with the desire to be *for* its members, Sisters in Crime redoubled its efforts toward networking, publicizing its members' work, and lending mutual support.

The purpose of Sisters in Crime is to combat discrimination against women in the mystery field, educate publishers and the general public as to inequalities in the treatment of female authors, and raise the level of awareness of their contribution to the field.

Membership in Sisters in Crime is open to all persons worldwide who have a special interest in mystery writing and in furthering the purposes of Sisters in Crime.

For more information about the Sisters in Crime national organization, please contact:

M. Beth Wasson, Executive Secretary
P.O. Box 442124
Lawrence, KS 66044-8933
(785) 842-1325
fax (785)-842-1034
email: sistersincrime@juno.com
website: www.sistersincrime.org
Books in Print http://www.books.com/sinc/authors.htm
http://www.books.com/sinc/yajuv.htm

The Los Angeles Chapter of Sisters in Crime is dedicated to promoting published and pre-published writers. With your support, we can offer new programs to meet this goal and continue to fund projects such as our anthology mystery recipe book and the No Crime Unpublished© Writers' Conference.

For more information about the Los Angeles Chapter of Sisters in Crime, please contact:

Sisters in Crime
Los Angeles Chapter
P.O. Box 251646
Los Angeles, CA 90025
(213) 694-2972
website: http://www.sistersincrimela.com

"Never underestimate the power of ...
a Sister in Crime."—GTK

Other titles by members of SinC/LA:

Desserticide aka Desserts Worth Dying For,
editors: Claire Carmichael McNab, Paulette Mouchet,
and Mary Terrill, 1995

Murder by Thirteen, SinC/LA anthology,
editors: Priscilla English, Lisa Seidman, Mae Woods, 1997

A Deadly Dozen, SinC/LA anthology,
editors: Susan Casmier, Aljean Harmetz,
Cynthia Lawrence. 2000

Introduction

Get ready to sink your teeth into a marvelous mixture of tasty recipes, forensic know-how, and other ingredients guaranteed to whet any mystery lover's appetite. Once again, the Los Angeles Chapter of Sisters in Crime has put a fabulous cookbook together. If you have the previous edition of *Desserticide*, you have an inkling of what's in store for you. This version is delightfully expanded and all the more fun.

Like its contributors, it's clever and original, and you'll find that it won't just satisfy your hunger, it will appeal to your sense of humor and your curiosity about the work of modern crime-solvers.

The last time this talented chapter collected favorite recipes and interspersed them with clues for those who read or write mysteries, I wasn't sure whether to keep it in my kitchen, in my office or on my nightstand for a little late-night reading. I have at last figured out what I'll do with this new collection—I'm buying three copies.

—Jan Burke

Editors Note

Jan Burke is the author of the novels *Goodnight, Irene; Sweet Dreams, Irene; Dear Irene; Remember Me, Irene; Hocus, Liar,* and *Bones.* Her novels have received three Agatha nominations and an Anthony nomination. Jan has also won the Macavity Award and the Ellery Queen Mystery Readers Award, as well as being the first woman to win first place for the EQMM Award. In 1999, her short story "Two Bits" received an Anthony Award nomination. Jan's novel, *Bones,* has been nominated for an Edgar Award for Best Novel. She is a member of the Los Angeles Chapter of Sisters in Crime as well as the President of the Mystery Writers of America/SoCal Chapter.

RECIPE TABLE OF CONTENTS

ALIBI LEMON ALMOND CAKE

1 box yellow cake mix
1 box 4-oz. instant lemon pudding
4 eggs
½ cup vegetable oil
¾ cup water
¼ cup margarine, melted and cooled
2 tsp. almond extract
½ box powdered sugar
Juice of 2 lemons

In a large mixing bowl, combine cake mix, gelatin, unbeaten eggs, oil, water, margarine and almond extract. Beat 10 minutes at medium speed. Pour into greased and floured tube pan. Bake at 325° for 50 to 60 minutes. Mix powdered sugar and lemon juice and heat. Pour hot glaze over warm cake in pan; allow to remain in pan to cool.

Favorite recipe of Billy The Kid. "Forget your six guns, pardner—go buy a *Desserticide* and get your own alibi."

Arrival of the Law at the Scene of the Crime

FBI statistics show that the faster law enforcement officers respond to a crime and begin preliminary investigations, the better the "solve" rate.

A thoughtful murderer will ensure that investigators are delayed as much as possible. This can be achieved by concealing the body, or ensuring that your victim is discovered after considerable time has passed.

When reporting the death yourself, it can be advantageous to give the wrong address (you always have the excuse that you were confused and upset) to delay arrival of the authorities.

"You can't tell a book by its cover, unless it's written by a Sister in Crime."

"A woman's place is on the best seller's list."

"Get revenge, but only in your books."

—GTK

AN ARRESTING CHOCOLATE CAKE
So easy, you can make it with one arm handcuffed to a post!

½ cup(1 stick) butter
1 cup sugar
4 large eggs
1 16-oz. can Hershey brand chocolate syrup
1 cup flour, sifted
1 tsp. baking powder
1 tsp. vanilla
Powdered sugar (optional)

Preheat oven to 350°. Grease and flour a tube pan.
Cream butter and sugar. Beat in eggs one at a time. Stir in chocolate syrup (it's the liquid). Fold in flour and baking powder. Beat at low speed. Stir in vanilla. Bake 40 to 50 minutes or until a toothpick inserted in center comes out clean. Cool 10 minutes. Turn out on rack and cool.

To gild the lily, sprinkle with confectioner's sugar before it is completely cool.

Favorite recipe of Susan B. Casmier, author of *The Body Politic*, past editor of *Ransom Notes*, editor of SinC/LA anthology, *A Deadly Dozen* and a past member of the Board of Directors.

The Crime Scene

The first priority of police officers at a crime scene is to preserve the area from any possible contamination and to keep all physical evidence from being altered or destroyed.

Of course, your intention as a murderer is precisely the opposite. For this reason, it is advisable to encourage as many people as possible to enter the crime scene prior to the arrival of the authorities. Neighbors, friends, and relatives can be called. A quick anonymous call to the media may be useful. Once the police arrive, demand a religious advisor and/ or doctor.

Always remember that the more people who enter a crime scene, the more compromised the evidence (against you) will be!

ANNIHILATION APPLE CAKE

1 cup walnuts, chopped
2 cups sugar
¾ cup oil
2 large eggs
1 tsp. vanilla
2 cups flour
1 tsp. baking soda
¼ tsp. salt
2 tsp. cinnamon

Preheat oven to 350°. Grease a 9x13-inch cake pan.

Cream together sugar, oil, eggs, and vanilla. Sift in flour, baking soda, salt, and cinnamon. Mix well. Stir in apples and walnuts. Turn into cake pan. Bake 45 minutes until toothpick inserted in center comes out clean. Cool.

Favorite recipe of Mae Woods, television producer of *When Danger Follows You Home*, screenwriter *for Tales from the Crypt*, editor of *Murder By Thirteen* anthology; and a SinC/LA Board of Directors member.

Evidence

There are two classes of evidence: direct and circumstantial. An eyewitness provides direct evidence. Circumstantial evidence relates to facts from which it may be inferred that a crime has been committed.

Hearsay evidence, something one has heard secondhand, is usually inadmissible, though exceptions include confessions or dying declarations. Witnesses must stick to the facts as they know them and avoid personal opinions or assumptions. The only exception to this is in the case of expert witnesses who are permitted to give their informed opinions.

If you do your job right, only sheer bad luck could lead to direct evidence against you. In the case of circumstantial evidence, familiarization with forensic science and careful planning should suffice.

ASSASSINATION APPLE CAKE
Will disguise just about any deadly dose.

½ cup flour, sifted
¾ cup brown sugar, firmly packed
1 tsp. baking powder
¼ tsp. salt
Dash of cinnamon
1 large egg
½ tsp. vanilla
1 cup apples, chopped
½ cup walnuts, chopped

Preheat oven to 350°. Grease an 8-inch cake pan.

Mix together flour, brown sugar, baking powder, salt, and cinnamon.

Stir in egg and vanilla and mix well. Fold in apples and walnuts. The batter will be stiff, almost like drop-cookie dough. Spread batter in cake pan and bake 25 to 30 minutes.

Favorite recipe of Mary T. Johnson, a long-time and faithful SinC/LA member.

Interrogation Techniques:
Good Guy-Bad Guy

Anyone who watches television is aware of the good guy-bad guy interrogation technique, which works well, especially with first-time offenders.

Two investigators are needed, one playing the "rogue cop," the other, "considerate and understanding." They work hard to give the impression that there is real conflict between them. When the rogue cop walks out of the interrogation room and slams the door, the "good cop" shows sympathy and kindness, often inducing the unsuspecting murderer to confide more than intended.

Do not fall for this scenario. It is always a set-up. Both investigators are working to have you incriminate yourself.

CHOCOLATE SHRIEK CAKE

1 cup plus 2 tbsp. salted butter
2 tbsp. salted butter
7 ozs. semi-sweet chocolate*
2 ozs. bitter chocolate
6 eggs eggs
½ cup granulated sugar
3/8 cup brown sugar
3/8 cup cake flour
3 tbsp. finely grated almonds
½ tsp. cream of tartar
*Use the best quality semisweet chocolate you can buy.

Butter the sides and bottom of an 8- or 9-inch spring-form pan. Line the bottom with baking parchment or waxed paper and flour the pan. Melt the butter in a large heavy-bottomed pan. Chop the chocolate in coarse pieces and add to the butter. Stir constantly over low heat until just melted and smooth; be careful not to overheat or the chocolate will turn grainy—it should not get much hotter than 115°. Set aside.

Separate the eggs and beat the sugars into the egg yolks until just mixed. While the chocolate is still warm, whisk the egg mixture into it, then stir in the flour and the almonds. If the combined mixture has cooled, warm it over low heat, stirring constantly, until it is barely warm. Warm the eggs whites slightly by swirling them in a bowl above a gas flame or over hot water—the eggs will beat to a greater volume when warmed. Add the cream of tartar to the egg whites and beat until they look creamy and form rounded peaks; if they look at all flaky they are overbeaten. Spread the egg whites over the chocolate mixture and fold them together quickly without deflating the whites. Pour into the prepared pan and bake at 375° for 30 to 40 minutes, or until the cake is completely set around the sides but still has a soft and creamy circle, about 6 inches across, in the center. The cake will rise and crack around the edge and separate from the softer center. The center should wiggle just slightly when you shake the pan gently; it will continue to cook when you take it out of the oven. Cool thoroughly in the pan.

To serve the cake, turn it out, peel the paper off the bottom, and powder lightly with powdered sugar. The cake keeps very well, if not iced, for three or four days. Do not refrigerate or freeze, just cover the pan with foil until ready to use. It's also good with ice cream or simple whipped cream.

Favorite recipe of Torene Svitil, author of numerous newspaper and magazine articles about film; SinC/LA Board of Directors; "No Crime Unpublished Conference©" Director; and author of "Nothing Now Can Ever Come to Any Good" in *Murder by Thirteen* anthology.

"You may be a day late and a dollar short—but not when you sell your book."—GTK

COUP DE GRÂCE BLACK RUSSIAN BOOZE CAKE

¼ cup Kahlua (coffee liqueur)
¼ cup Vodka
1 pkg. yellow cake mix
1 small pkg. instant chocolate pudding
4 eggs
1 cup vegetable oil
¾ cup water

Blend all ingredients for 2 minutes at medium speed. Bake in a Bundt pan at 350° for 45 to 50 minutes.

Favorite recipe of Wayne Tappon, author of six short stories for *Alfred Hitchcock's Mystery Magazine*, including "To Rob a Bank" and "Doggie and Weenie"; SinC/LA Board of Directors 1998-2002; and has a hidden talent for producing the best chili in the world.

Death by Turtling
A common sailing term for the action of a sailing boat
when running before a high sea, it slews around inadvert-
ently broadside on the waves, and turns completely upside
down with the sail tip pointed toward the bottom of the
ocean. It's an expensive way of "doing in an ol' sea salt."

> "It's easier and more profitable for the perp
> to give the victim several Margueritas and
> wait for him to fall overboard."—DJB

> "Still waters run deep—over a body."—GTK

> "An idle mind is ... not reading a mystery."
> —GTK

DEATH BY TURTLE

1 box German chocolate cake mix
2 cups soft caramels
1 cup sweetened condensed milk
1 cube margarine
1 cup chocolate chips
1 cup coarsely chopped pecans

Grease and flour 9x13 glass dish.

Prepare cake mix as described. Pour ½ batter (2½ cups) into glass dish and bake at 325° for 30 minutes. Melt caramels, milk, and margarine in microwave on high for 6 minutes.

Pour melted caramel mix over baked portion of cake. Sprinkle chocolate chips and pecans evenly over caramel mix. Pour remaining uncooked cake batter on top and bake 50 minutes at 325°. Let cool before cutting.

Favorite recipe of Dr. Gay Toltl Kinman, author of preface to *The Catalog of the Los Angeles Police Dept. Library*, playwright, "The Wicked Well"; editor of *Desserticide II, aka Just Desserts and Deathly Advice*, contributor of "Miss Parker and the Cutter-Sanborn Tables" in the SinC/LA anthology, *A Deadly Dozen*, and has published numerous articles in professional women's, governmental, library, police, law, writing and political publications, and press releases in newspapers. SinC/LA Board of Directors since 1996.

What An Antacid Way To Go

Researchers for the Food and Drug Administration warn that gulping down mouthfuls of indigestion remedies may be fatal.

Excessive use of antacids may lead to magnesium poisoning. Symptoms can include weakness, drowsiness, confusion, clumsiness, paralysis, and coma.

As a means of murder, magnesium poisoning would be difficult to prove. This is a suitable poison if you are a very bad cook: make your dessert even less digestible than usual, then encourage your victim to consume vast quantities of antacid.

FOUL PLAY SPONGE CAKE

12 eggs, separated
2 cups sugar
2/3 cup matzo cake meal
1/3 cup potato starch
Juice of 1 lemon

Beat egg whites stiff.

Add sugar gradually to egg whites and mix.

In a separate bowl, beat egg yolks then add lemon juice and pour yolk and lemon juice into egg whites.

Very slowly, add dry ingredients (starch and matzo) so there are no lumps in mixture. Spray with Pam® or coat tube cake pan with oil.

Pour mixture into tube pan and bake at 350° for one hour. To test if done, place a toothpick in the center and see if it is dry. Let cake cool ten minutes. Loosen edges with a knife then turn upside down onto a plate to completely cool.

Favorite recipe of Lois Hirt, author for a national professional journal; columnist; newspaper interviewer and reviewer.

If You Are Unlucky Enough To Be Arrested

You have the right to remain silent. You do not have to answer any questions, but you may decide that a cooperative stance will be to your advantage.

Any statement you make (spoken or written) can be used against you.

You have the right to speak with an attorney and to have an attorney present when you are questioned.

If you want, but can't afford, an attorney, one must be provided without charge before any interrogation can begin.

Important: Take careful note of whether you have been advised of your Miranda rights when taken into custody. If you have not had your rights read to you, do *not* point this out. Anything you say or do will be inadmissible in a court of law!

GET YOUR HANDS UPSIDE-DOWN CAKE

1 tbsp. butter
1 tbsp. grated fresh ginger
1 1/3 cups brown sugar, divided
1 15-oz. can juice-packed peaches
1 Egg
1 egg white
1/3 cup oil
½ cup milk
1½ tsp. vanilla extract
1½ cups unbleached flour
Pinch of salt
1½ tsp. baking powder

Preheat oven to 375°. Place butter in a 9-inch cake pan and put in oven until butter melts. Add ginger and 1/3 cup sugar. Mix and distribute evenly in pan. Drain peaches, reserving ¾ cup juice. Cut peaches into 1-inch slices and arrange in pan. Set aside. In a medium bowl, combine egg, egg white, oil, ¾ of reserved peach juice, and the milk and vanilla. In another bowl, mix remaining sugar, flour, salt and baking powder.

Gradually add dry ingredients to wet. Pour mixture evenly over peaches. Bake about 30 minutes, or until a toothpick inserted into cake (not fruit) comes out clean. Cool in pan on a wire rack. Turn out onto a plate to serve.

Favorite recipe of Angela Hynes, author of *A Guide to Aphrodisiacs and Sexual Pleasures* with Cynthia Watson, M.D., and *The Pleasures of Afternoon Tea*, and several others; SinC/LA Vice President, 2000-2002.

Malice Aforethought

Murder is defined as "the unlawful killing of a human being with malice aforethought." Malice aforethought is the deliberate intention to unlawfully take away the life of someone else.

Although the term gives the impression that you have planned the death of your victim, this is not the case. In contrast to accidental death, malice aforethought simply means that you had intent to do your victim harm that could result in death.

Be aware that the use of poison shows deliberate premeditation and so fulfills the requirements of malice aforethought. Find an explanation for how the poison accidentally appeared in your victim's dessert.

HACK AND CHOP APRICOT COCONUT CAKE

Cake:
1 pkg yellow cake mix
1 16oz. can apricots (do not drain)
¾ cup Angel Flake® coconut
2 eggs
½ cup firmly packed brown sugar

Combine cake mix, apricots with syrup, and coconut flakes in a large mixing bowl. Blend, then beat at medium speed for 2 minutes. Pour into a 9x13 pan. Sprinkle with brown sugar. Bake at 325° for 45 minutes or until cake springs back. Start the topping while cake is baking. Pour topping onto the hot cake while in the pan. Cake is a little too moist to turn out of pan onto a plate.

Topping:
¾ lb. butter
½ cup granulated sugar
½ cup evaporated milk
¾ cups Angel Flake® coconut

Bring butter, granulated sugar and evaporated milk to a boil: boil on low for 2 minutes. Remove pan from heat and stir in coconut. Set aside. Apply directly onto hot cake and leave in the pan.

> Favorite recipe of Wayne Tappon, author of six short stories *in Alfred Hitchcock's Mystery Magazine*, including "To Rob a Bank" and "Doggie and Weenie"; SinC/LA Board of Directors 1998-2000; and has a hidden talent for producing the best chili in the world.

The Perfect Murder

The perfect murder is not one where no one is ever tried and found guilty of the crime—that could be described as a wholly successful murder.

The truly perfect murder is the one that is never seen as a murder in the first place. We can never know this, but perhaps a multitude of unknown murderers walk among us, smiling mildly as they contemplate their lethal achievements.

"Oh, what a tangled web we weave,
When first we practice to deceive!"—Sir Walter Scott, *Marmion*

"If all else fails—kill him."—GTK

I DIDN'T DO IT! PEANUT BUTTER FUDGE CAKE

2 cups boiling water
4 1-oz. squares unsweetened baking chocolate
2 cups sugar
2/3 cup butter or margarine, softened
2 large eggs
2 tsp. vanilla
3 cups flour
1 tsp. baking powder
1½ tsp. baking soda
1 cup semi-sweet chocolate chips
1 cup peanut butter chips

Chocolate Glaze and Peanut Butter recipes follow:

Preheat oven to 350°. Grease a 12-cup Bundt pan.
Pour boiling water over unsweetened chocolate. Do not stir. Set aside; cool to lukewarm. Cream sugar and butter until smooth. Beat in eggs and vanilla. Drain water from chocolate, reserving liquid. Blend melted chocolate into creamed mixture. Combine flour, baking powder, and baking soda. Add to creamed mixture alternately with reserved liquid from chocolate. Beat thoroughly at low speed after each addition. Stir in chocolate and peanut butter chips. Turn into pan. Bake 50 to 55 minutes or until toothpick inserted in center comes out clean.

Cool 15 minutes; remove from pan. Cool completely before glazing. Spoon Chocolate Glaze over entire cake. Refrigerate until glaze is firm. Drizzle with Peanut Butter Glaze. Refrigerate.

Chocolate Glaze
¼ cup (½ stick) margarine or butter
2 tbsp. water

3 tbsp. light corn syrup
2 tsp. vanilla
1 cup semi-sweet chocolate chips
¼ cup powdered sugar, sifted

In medium saucepan; combine margarine, water, corn syrup, and vanilla. Heat to boiling. Add chocolate chips. Cover and remove from heat. Let stand 5 minutes. Remove lid. Stir mixture until smooth. Stir in powdered sugar until blended. Chill 10 minutes or until glaze is of spreading consistency.

Peanut Butter Glaze
¾ cup powdered sugar, sifted
2 tbsp. peanut butter
2 to 3 tbsp. hot whipping cream or milk

In small bowl blend powdered sugar, peanut butter, and cream.

> Favorite recipe of Lisa Seidman, TV scriptwriter for "Falcon Crest," "Dallas," "Cagney & Lacey," "Murder, She Wrote," "Knots Landing," and "Sunset Beach." Editor of *Murder by Thirteen*, author of "Over My Shoulder" in the SinC/LA anthology, *A Deadly Dozen.*

IT'S A JAILBREAK ... SQUASH ME CAKE WITH CELL BLOCK 7 FROSTING

3, 6" zucchinis, shredded
1 cup brown sugar
½ cup white sugar
½ cup cold butter, in chunks
3 eggs
1 tsp. vanilla
½ cup buttermilk
2½ cups flour
½ tsp. cinnamon
½ tsp. allspice
½ tsp. salt
2 tsp. baking soda
¼ cup cocoa
4 ozs. chocolate chips

Shred zucchini in a large bowl and set aside. In another bowl, cream eggs, vanilla and buttermilk and set aside. Measure into sifter: flour, allspice, cinnamon, salt, baking soda and cocoa.

Fold dry mixture and creamed mix into the shredded zucchini. Mix by hand. Pour into greased and floured 9x13 baking pan. Sprinkle with 4 ozs. (¾ cup) chocolate chips on top and bake at 325° for 45 minutes.

CELL BLOCK 7 FROSTING:
¼ lb. butter or margarine
¾ cup sugar
2 squares unsweetened chocolate, melted
1 tsp. vanilla
2 eggs

Cream butter and sugar until light and fluffy. Add melted chocolate and vanilla. Beat until smooth. Add eggs, one at a time, beating for 5 minutes after each egg. *Chill before spreading on cake.*

Favorite recipe of The Bird Man of Alcatraz.

"An honorable murder, if you will:
For naught I did in hate, but all in honor."—
Shakespeare: *Othello*, Act IV, Scene 3

"Everybody is a potential murderer. I've never killed anyone, but I frequently get satisfaction reading the obituary notices."—Clarence Darrow in an interview

MISS MARPLE'S MILKY WAY CAKE

Cake:
8 Milky Way® candy bars
½ cup butter or margarine, melted
2 cups sugar
½ cup butter or margarine, softened
4 eggs
1 tsp. vanilla extract
1¼ cups buttermilk
½ tsp. baking soda
3 cups all-purpose flour
1 cup pecans, chopped medium

Combine candy bars and ½ cup melted butter or margarine in sauce pan. Place over low heat until candy bars are melted, stirring constantly; cool. Cream sugar and ½ cup softened butter until light and fluffy. Add eggs, one at a time, beating well, after each addition. Stir in vanilla extract. Combine buttermilk and soda. Add to creamed mixture, alternating flour, and beating well after each addition. Stir in candy bar mixture with pecans. Pour into greased and floured 10-inch tube pan. Bake at 325° for 1 hour and 20 minutes or until done.

Let cool in pan 1 hour. Remove from pan and complete cooling on wire rack.

Milk Chocolate Frosting:
2½ cups sugar
1 cup evaporated milk, undiluted
½ cup butter or margarine, melted
1 6-oz. pkg. semi-sweet chocolate bits
1 cup marshmallow cream

Combine sugar, milk, and butter in heavy sauce pan.

Cook over medium heat until small amount dropped in cold water forms a soft ball. Remove from heat. Add chocolate bits and marshmallow cream, stirring until melted.

> Favorite recipe of Gayle Pfaucht, editor of SinC/LA newsletter, *Ransom Notes* and Board member 1998-2002. She is currently writing a mystery series.

"Alibis are worth a dime a dozen unless they're good ones."—GTK

SHAKY ALIBI APPLE CRUMBLE

4 cups Granny Smith apples, peeled and sliced
½ cup brown sugar
½ cup flour
2 tbsp. lemon juice
½ cup (1 stick) butter or margarine
1 tsp. cinnamon

Preheat oven to 350 °. Lightly butter a glass baking dish.
Spread apple slices evenly over bottom of baking dish.
Sprinkle lemon juice over apple slices. Cream together butter and brown sugar. Stir in flour and cinnamon until mixture is crumbly. Spread over the apples. Bake 30 minutes.
Serve warm or cold.

Favorite recipe of Mae Woods, television producer of *When Danger Follows You Home*, screenwriter for *Tales from the Crypt*, editor of *Murder by Thirteen* anthology; and a SinC/LA Board of Directors member.

"Any gun will do—for a random shot."—DJB

"Free advice is exactly what it's worth—unless it's in this book." —GTK

"When in doubt—do a foul deed."—GTK

"Blood, though it sleep a time, yet never dies. The gods on murtherers fix revengeful eyes."—*The Widdowes Tears* by George Chapman

SMOKIN' PISTOL PINEAPPLE PUDDING CAKE

1 yellow cake baked according to directions
1 4-oz. can crushed pineapple
1 cup sugar
One 6-oz. pkg. vanilla pudding mix (not instant)
1 cup whipping cream
Coconut, lightly toasted (according to taste)

Bake cake mix in a 9x13 pan.
Combine pineapple and sugar. Bring to a boil, then cool slightly. Poke holes in baked cake with fork. Pour pineapple mix over cake. Prepare vanilla pudding and cool. Spread pudding on top of cake. Chill in refrigerator. Before serving, top with whipped cream and coconut.

Favorite recipe of Gayle Pfaucht, editor of SinC/LA newsletter, *Ransom Notes*. Board member 1998-2002. She is currently working on a mystery series about a hypnotist.

Cyanide

Potassium cyanide (prussic acid) acts very rapidly and is popular as a means of suicide. It occurs as a plot device in many spy novels—rather than confess under torture, the spy bites on the capsule hooked over his or her molars. It was also the chosen method of suicide for Nazi war criminals Goring and Himmler.

Occurring naturally in stone fruits (within the kernel), such as the cherry and peach, it has a characteristic odor of bitter almonds. With a fatal dose, death occurs within four to five minutes as the respiratory center in the brain shuts down. In the form of prussic acid, it can kill within seconds.

Poisoners should delay official examination of victims, as cyanide changes chemically in the body and may be difficult to detect after time.

SNEAK ATTACK CARROT CAKE
With five (count 'em!) deadly spices

1½ cups sugar
1 tbsp. molasses
4 large eggs
2 cups flour
1 tsp. baking powder
1 tsp. baking soda
½ tsp. salt
2 tsp. cinnamon
½ tsp. ginger
½ tsp. cloves
¼ tsp. nutmeg
¼ tsp. cardamon
¾ cup oil
3 cups grated carrots
½ cup raisins
2/3 cup walnuts, chopped
Watch Your Back Frosting (recipe follows)

Preheat oven to 350°. Oil and flour one angel food cake pan, or one 9x13-inch cake pan, or two 8-inch layer pans.

Mix sugar, molasses, and eggs together with wire whisk. Sift the dry ingredients and stir into sugar mixture. Add ½ cup oil and the carrots and mix well. Add raisins, walnuts, and remaining oil, mixing well again. Pour batter into cake pan or pans. Bake 60 to 75 minutes for the large pans or 40 to 55 minutes for small pans. Cool 10 minutes. Turn out on rack and cool. Dust with powdered sugar or frost with Watch Your Back Frosting.

WATCH YOUR BACK FROSTING
4 ozs. cream cheese
2 tbsp. butter

1 ½ cups powdered sugar
1 tbsp. cream
1 tsp. vanilla, brandy or rum

Combine cream cheese, butter, powdered sugar, cream, and flavoring. Beat until smooth. Spread on cake.

> Favorite recipe of Gayle McGary Partlow author of short stories in the SinC/LA anthologies, *Murder by Thirteen* and *A Deadly Dozen*. Ms. Partlow created the artwork for the cover of the first edition of *Murder by Thirteen,* and for the SinC/LA logo. Currently Gayle is a SinC/LA member of the Board of Directors and layout editor for *Ransom Notes.*

Ugly Way To Die Lemon Pecan Cake

1 pkg. white cake mix
1 pkg. lemon instant pudding
¾ cup salad oil
4 eggs
1 cup sour cream
1 tsp. cinnamon
½ cup sugar
½ cup crushed pecans

Mix pudding, cake mix, oil, eggs and sour cream and beat 4 minutes. Pour half of batter in greased tube pan. Mix sugar, cinnamon, pecans in a separate bowl. Sprinkle first layer of batter with the mixture. Pour remaining batter on top then pour the other half of the cinnamon mixture to finish. Bake 350° 45-55 minutes.

Favorite recipe of Sherlock Holmes and Professor Moriarty at Victoria Falls.

Remember, Eat Your Words

With his final breath the victim stated that the shooter was "Spanky from La Puente." Though the investigators and the prosecutors had not been able to connect that moniker to him based on other evidence, a gang member was brought to trial.

One morning the bailiff went to the holding cell to retrieve the young man for court that day. In the defendant's possession was a note he had written to another inmate. The note was signed "Spanky La Puente." The bailiff recognizing the importance of the moniker used as the signature, dashed into the courtroom and quickly returned to the holding cell with the Deputy DA.

Despite their speed, by the time they returned to the cell the signature had been torn off from the note in question. In the opposite corner of the cell lay thirty pieces of "confetti" which were gingerly collected and brought with the note to the Questioned Documents section of the crime lab. The "confetti" was reconstructed to complete the signature area of the note. This final piece of evidence assured a successful prosecution of the defendant. Perhaps next time this fellow will know to "eat his words."

Contributed by Barbara L. Torres, Forensic Document Examiner/Questioned Document Section of the Los Angeles County Sheriff's Dept./Scientific Services Bureau.

WHAT A WAY TO DIE SOUR CREAM CHOCOLATE CAKE
Chocolate lovers will dream of this!

3 cups cake flour
3 cups sugar
¾ cup cocoa
¾ cup (1½ sticks) butter, softened
¾ cup sour cream
1½ cups hot water
2¼ tsp. baking soda
3 large eggs
2 tsp. vanilla
1 can ready-made sour cream chocolate frosting

Preheat oven to 350°. Line one 11x16-inch cake pan or two oversized 10-inch round cake pans with waxed paper. (This batter won't fit in regular-size pans—the cake turns our very high and moist.)

Dissolve baking soda in the hot water and set aside. Sift the flour and set aside. Sift sugar into mixer bowl. Add cocoa, butter, and sour cream. Blend at medium speed; make sure beaters are in sour cream so cocoa won't fly.

Add the eggs one at a time to sour cream mixture, beating well after each addition. Add vanilla. Reduce speed to low. Alternately beat in flour and baking soda-water mixture. Batter will be runny. Pour batter into cake pan. Bake 45 to 50 minutes until toothpick inserted in center comes out clean. Cool. Frost with ready-made sour cream chocolate frosting.

Favorite recipe of Kevin Gillogly, contributing author to SinC/LA anthology *Murder by Thirteen*, and advertising writer. As a former *sous chef*, he discovered long ago a thickening roux is as vital to the culinary arts as plot thickening is to a good mystery. SinC/LA Board of Directors, 2000-2002.

A Crook's Gastronomic Delight

Writers should understand that burglary is hard work. Perps often work up quite an appetite while laboring about the crime scene discovering goodies for the future resale to their local fence or swap meet. It is common to find foodstuffs and beverages strewn about the premises that gave evidence to both the bad guy's food favorite and prints, both finger and tooth.

A notable case of mine is the "bologna on the refrigerator caper" wherein a dastardly house vandal greedily chomped this popular meat substitute. He generously left the remains in plain sight on the refrigerator for later forensic analysis. His teeth were as crooked as his intentions thereby rendering the cliché "You are what you eat" an apt phrase.

Mike Bowers, DDS, Forensic odontologist, forensic writer, lawyer, certified crime scene analyst and flying instructor on the weekends.

BLACKMAILER'S BRITTLE

1 cup sugar
½ cup light corn syrup
Dash of salt
1 to 1½ cups shelled raw Spanish peanuts (or combination
of hazlenuts and almonds— my favorite)
1 tablespoon margarine or butter
1½ tsp. baking soda
1 tsp. vanilla

Grease baking sheet heavily. Mix sugar, syrup and salt
in 3-qt. glass casserole. Stir in peanuts. Microwave on High
about 8 to 10 minutes, stirring twice until light brown. Must
be watched so it will not brown too much. Remove from
microwave and stir in butter, soda and vanilla—quickly—
and stir until foamy.

Quickly spread on baking sheet as thin as possible. I find
that greasing the spoon helps in spreading. Cool. Break into
pieces and *enjoy*.

Favorite recipe of R.A. Forster, author of *Be-
yond Malice, Character Witness, The Men-
tor*, and the *USA Today* bestseller, *Keeping
Counsel.*

Feigning Insanity to Avoid a Murder Rap

It is wise to research the particular form of madness you will be using. Symptoms you might consider developing include:

Delirium—showing disorganized thinking: you ramble, make incoherent comments, and generally indicate that you have great difficulty in maintaining attention on what is going on around you.

Dementia—your ability to think is seriously impaired, particularly your judgment and abstract thought processes.

Behavior that indicates you are suffering from delusions and hallucinations is always useful.

Special Note: Unsporting prosecutors will try to trap you into showing sanity. Be consistent. Know your madness and stick to it!

MYSTERIOUS PECAN MADNESS

1 cup firmly packed brown sugar
1 cup granulated sugar
1 tbsp. light corn syrup
1 tbsp. butter
5 tbsp. water
2½ cups whole pecans
A few sheets wax paper

Bring to a boil, stirring occasionally. When the mixture reaches the "soft ball stage," mix in whole pecans. Remove from heat, stir. Drop small spoonfuls onto wax paper. Let cool then store in airtight container with a sheet of wax paper between each layer.

Can be used for a card party, dinner party or a fat attack.

Favorite recipe of Diane Jay Bouchard, author of nonfiction magazine and newspaper articles, and editor of *Desserticide II, aka Just Desserts and Deathly Advice.* SinC/LA Vice President 1995-1997 and President 1997-2002.

The Alibi

The word alibi is Latin for "elsewhere" and is a favored defense in both fiction and real life. An alibi is used to establish that you could not possibly have committed the crime because you were somewhere else at the time.

Take care if you ask someone to lie to establish your alibi—it's amazing how the threat of prosecution can encourage even your nearest and dearest to tell the inconvenient truth.

Another common problem is blackmail. The person providing your alibi correctly assumes that you have a keen interest in maintaining the deception and demands payment to keep quiet. In a worst-case scenario, you would be forced to commit yet another murder and go to the trouble of establishing a new alibi.

THE BIG SLEEP SCONES

2 ½ cups all-purpose flour
2 tsp. baking powder
1 tsp. baking soda
½ tsp. salt
½ cup sugar
6 tbsp. cold butter, cut in small pieces
½ cup raisins
1 egg, beaten
Grated peel of ½ lemon
1 8-oz. carton plain yogurt
Milk for brushing on scones

Preheat oven to 425°. Lightly grease a large cookie sheet. Sift flour, baking powder, baking soda and salt into a large bowl. Stir in sugar. With your fingers, rub in butter pieces until mixture is crumbly. Add raisins. With a fork, stir in egg and lemon peel. Add yogurt, a little at a time, to make a dry dough that barely holds together (you may not use all the yogurt.). Turn dough out onto a floured surface. Roll out with a floured rolling pin to about ½-inch thick. Cut into rounds with a 1½-inch cookie cutter. Place on cookie sheet and brush tops with milk. Bake 10 to 12 minutes, or until scones are well risen and golden. Cool on a wire rack for 5 minutes. Split, and serve warm with butter, jam or lemon curd.

Favorite recipe of Angela Hynes, author of *A Guide to Aphrodiasiacs and Sexual Pleasures,* with Cynthia Watson M.D., and *The Pleasures of Afternoon Tea* and several others; SinC/ LA Vice President, 2000-2002.

Time of Death

Crime novels often give the impression that time of death is easy to ascertain. In reality, this is not the case, although there are factors that can be used to give an estimate.

For example, a dead body will cool by approximately 1.5°F/hour, reaching a uniform temperature with the environment after 24 hours. Lividity, staining caused by settling of the blood in the lower portions of the body, shows in 3-5 hours. Rigor mortis begins in 1-4 hours.

Be aware that, apart from rigor and lividity, stomach contents may be examined to determine how far digestion is advanced. So, make the final meal a memorable one!

BLOOD STREUSEL AND GORE COFFEECAKE
It oozes with "blood" and "innards" when you slice it!

1 cup (2 sticks) butter or margarine, softened
1 cup sugar
4 large eggs
1¾ cups flour
2 tsp. baking powder
2 tsp. grated lemon peel
1 1½-lb. can raspberry pie filling
1 1-lb. can sliced cling peaches, drained

Preheat oven to 325°. Grease and flour a 9x13-inch cake pan.

In a large bowl beat butter and sugar at medium speed until smooth and lemon-colored. Beat in eggs, one at a time. Sift together flour and baking powder and gradually beat into egg mixture. Beat in lemon peel. Spread batter evenly in cake pan. Arrange peaches on top. Spread raspberry pie filling over peaches. Top with Streusel Topping. Bake 45 to 50 minutes until light golden in color. Cut into squares.

Streusel Topping
½ cup butter or margarine
1 cup flour
¼ cup sugar

Melt the butter. Stir in flour and sugar to form soft dough. Pinch topping into tiny pieces and sprinkle over top of raspberry pie filling.

Favorite recipe of Judith K. Smith, author of a short story in SinC/LA anthology, *Murder by Thirteen*; past Board of Directors;"No Crime Unpublished©" Conference Director; and is currently writing a Bea Silver mystery.

"If once a man indulges himself in murder, very soon he comes to think little of robbing; and from robbing he next comes to drinking and Sabbath-breaking, and from that to in-civility and procrastination."—Thomas de Quincey: *Murder Considered as One of the Fine Arts*

"Don't put all your eggs in one basket—use several methods for murder."—GTK

Coroner's Surprise Banana Bread

1¾ cups sifted all-purpose flour
2¼ tsp. double-acting baking powder
1/3 cup regular salted butter
2/3 cup sugar
¾ tsp. grated lime zest or rind (the green bit only)
¼ tsp. grated orange zest or rind (the orange bit only)
1-2 eggs, beaten
2 cups mashed ripe bananas

Preheat oven to 350°. You will need 2 bowls, one small for dry ingredients and one large for wet ingredients. Sift together the flour and baking powder in the smaller bowl. Set the dry ingredients aside for the moment. Blend the butter and sugar together until creamy in the larger bowl. (You can do this in a food processor if desired). Beat the eggs and add to the butter and sugar mixture. Grate the lime and orange zest and add to butter and sugar mixture. Mix thoroughly. In a two-cup measure start mashing the bananas into a pulp; bananas should be ripe and a bit mushy. For the best flavor, try to find some of the exotic tropical bananas such as manzano, lady fingers, or apple bananas. Regular bananas will work fine, but won't be quite as tasty. Once the two-cup measure is full of mashed bananas (it is okay to have some recognizable banana chunks), mix the bananas into the other wet ingredients in the large bowl.

Add the sifted flour and baking powder into the wet ingredients in about three parts, mixing well after each portion is added. Mix the batter thoroughly. Grease a bread or loaf pan and pour the mixture into the pan. Bake the bread about 1 hour until the top is golden brown and a toothpick stuck in the center comes out clean. Cool the bread on a wire rack before slicing and devouring.

Sweet Banana Bread Variation: If you prefer a sweeter bread, leave out the lime and orange zest and add ½ cup chocolate chips and/or ½ cup broken walnuts.

> Favorite recipe of Jamie Wallace, contributing author, "Driven to Kill" in the SinC/LA anthology, *A Deadly Dozen*, and Conference Director, "No Crime Unpublished©." Board of Directors 1996, and Vice President 1997-1999.

"The reason for murder often lies as much in the murderee as in the dispatcher."—John Bonett and Emily Bonett, *The Sound of Murder*

"No stupid man ever suspected himself of being anything but clever."—Thomas Bailey Aldrich, *The Stillwater Tragedy*

"If poverty is the mother of all crimes, lack of intelligence is their father."—Jean de La Bryere, *Characters*

HIT WOMAN GINGERBREAD
You'll die happy

2 cups flour
2 tsp. baking powder
¼ tsp. baking soda
¼ tsp. salt
2 tsp. ground ginger
1 tsp. cinnamon
1/3 cup shortening or margarine
½ cup sugar
1 large egg
¾ cup molasses
¾ cup sour milk

Preheat oven to 350°. Grease an 8x8x2-inch cake pan. Thoroughly combine the flour, baking powder, soda, salt, and spices. Set aside. Cream shortening and sugar together. Add egg and beat until fluffy. Stir in molasses. Alternately add dry ingredients and sour milk, stirring gently until just blended. Batter will be thick. Turn into cake pan and make sure it fills the corners. Bake 45 to 50 minutes or until the bread springs back when gently pressed in the center.

Serve hot, warm, or cold, though cutting it nicely when hot takes a bit of practice. Top with whipped cream, ice cream, your favorite fruit sauce, or dust with powdered sugar.

Favorite recipe of Susan M. Stephenson, author of "How to Grow Orchids Outdoors in Southern California," in the *American Orchid Society Bulletin*, and other articles about orchids, and public relations materials; Board of Directors, 1995-2002 as secretary, membership chair; *Ransome Notes* editor; and *Murder by Thirteen* anthology committee member and PBS Pledge Drive Coordinator.

"Singularity is almost invariably a clue. The more featureless and commonplace a crime is, the more difficult it is to bring it home."— Arthur Conan Doyle, *The Adventures of Sherlock Holmes*

"Let bygones be bygones—after you've done him in."—GTK

OUT OF CONTROL YOGURT COFFEECAKE
Run amok with yogurt.

1 box (18½ ozs.) yellow cake mix (not pudding mix)
1 cup plain whole milk yogurt
½ cup water
2 large eggs
1 cup walnuts or pecans, chopped
2 tsp. ground cinnamon
½ cup sugar

Preheat oven according to cake mix package directions. Grease and flour a 9x13-inch cake pan.

Prepare cake mix according to package directions, substituting the yogurt for 1 cup water required in the box mix. Pour half the batter into the cake pan. Combine nuts, cinnamon, and sugar. Sprinkle half over the batter. Top with remaining batter and nut mixture. Bake according to package directions. Cool in the pan. This is a lighter version of sour cream coffeecake with 300 less calories!

Favorite recipe of Cynthia Lawrence, author of *Take-Out City*, editor of SinC/LA anthology, *A Deadly Dozen*, and a past Board of Directors member.

Beware Would-Be Arsonists
Arson is a frustrating method of crime. It draws attention to itself, it requires an immediate departure, it never fully obliterates what you hope to conceal and it leaves the firebug to either wallow in anonymity or to risk fame—and the proper consequences.

Contributed by Vicki L. Clawson, Senior Criminalist/Physical Evidence Section of the Los Angeles County Sheriff's Dept./Scientific Services Bureau

SWIFT DISPATCH APPLE BREAD

1 cup Wesson oil
2 cups sugar
2 eggs
3 cups sifted flour
2 tsp. baking powder
1 tbsp. vanilla
1 heaping tsp. cinnamon
3 cups chopped apples

Mix cinnamon into the apples, set aside. In another bowl mix oil and sugar, add 1 egg at a time, then alternate flour and apples into the mixture. Stir in vanilla whenever you feel like it. Bake in 2 greased loaf pans at 350° for about 1 hour.

Voilà—perfect apple bread.

Favorite recipe of C. J. Songer, author of *Bait*, and *Hook*.

"I came to the conclusion many years ago that almost all crime is due to the repressed desire for aesthetic expression."—Evelyn Waugh, *Decline and Fall*

"Never give a perpetrator an even break—unless it's his legs."—DJB

Amaretto Swoon Cheesecake

1 cup graham cracker crumbs
½ cup almonds, toasted and ground
¼ cup (½ stick) butter or margarine, melted
1/3 cup + 2 tbsp. sugar, divided
1/3 cup + 4 tbsp. Amaretto, divided
4 ozs. almond paste
2 tbsp. flour
3 8-oz. pkgs. cream cheese
4 large eggs, or equivalent egg substitute
1 cup sour cream, regular or imitation
Sliced almonds (optional)

Preheat oven to 350°. Grease a 9-inch springform pan.

Allow cream cheese to soften at room temperature. Combine graham cracker crumbs, ground almonds, butter, 1 tbsp. sugar, and 1 tbsp. Amaretto. Press crust mixture onto bottom and up the sides of pan. Refrigerate crust. Combine almond paste, 1/3 cup sugar, and flour. Beat until smooth. Add 1/3 cup Amaretto and beat. Add softened cream cheese, one package at a time, and beat in. Add 1 egg at a time and beat in and well until smooth. Pour batter into chilled crust. Bake 45 to 50 minutes. Cheesecake will not be fully set in center.

While cheesecake bakes, blend together sour cream, 3 tbspss Amaretto, and 1 tbsp. sugar. Spread mixture over top of baked cake. Return to oven for 20 minutes or until center is firm. Cool at room temperature on rack for 1 hour, then refrigerate in pan for 4 hours. To serve, remove sides of pan and garnish with sliced almonds.

Favorite recipe of Kris Neri, author of sixty short stories, and mystery novel, *Revenge of the Gypsy Queen*, Derringer Award winner for "L.A. Justice" in SinC/LA anthology *Murder by Thirteen*, and "Sentence Imposed" in *A Deadly Dozen;* SinC/LA Vice President 1994-1995 and President 1995-1997.

"Crimes, like virtues, are their own rewards."—George Farquhar, *The Inconstant*

"When you have a bee in your bonnet, you don't start swinging with a fly swatter."—Michael Avallone, *The Tall Delores*

"A bullet can give a man a terrific case of indigestion, frequently ending in a trip to the boneyard."—Robert Leslie Bellam, "Diamonds of Death," *Hollywood Detective*, August

"A penny-ante chiseler can get just as trigger-happy as a big timer."—Andrew Bergman, *The Big Kiss-Off*

"Death is a lonely business."—Ray Bradbury, *Death is a Lonely Business*

THE DEVIL MADE ME DO IT CHOCOLATE CHIP CHEESECAKE
Every forkful is to die for, each chocolate chip another
coffin nail to seal your victim's fate.

1 cup graham cracker crumbs
3 tbsp. sugar
3 tbsp. margarine or butter
3 8-oz. pkgs. cream cheese, softened
¾ cup sugar
3 large eggs
1 cup small semi-sweet chocolate chips
1 tsp. vanilla

Preheat oven to 450°.

Combine graham cracker crumbs, sugar, and margarine well. Press into the bottom of a 9-inch springform pan. Combine cream cheese and sugar at medium speed until well blended. Add eggs one at a time. Mix well. Add chocolate chips and vanilla. Pour over crust. Bake 10 minutes at 450°, then reduce heat to 250° and bake 35 minutes longer. Loosen cake from rim of pan. Cool before removing from pan. Chill before serving.

> Favorite recipe of Judith K. Smith, author of a short story in the SinC/LA anthology, *Murder by Thirteen*; past Board of Directors member; "No Crime Unpublished©" Conference Director; and is currently writing a Bea Silver Mystery.

Remodeling Can Be Hazardous To One's Health
A Victorian house undergoing remodeling is the setting
of this Halloween Eve homicide.

A headless torso was found in a playroom adjacent to
the garage. Investigators' search of the room revealed an
end table with a closed cabinet below. Inside was found a
round object covered with a sheepskin. Once the sheepskin
was peeled back (like an onion skin) a Mylar balloon with a
pumpkin face was exposed. The balloon was peeled back to
reveal a head. Herman's head looked peaceful and serene,
to be precise, belying the horrific events of his murder. Ironi-
cally, this gruesome discovery coincided with a popular
sitcom on nighttime television entitled "Herman's Head."

Story contributed by Gisele La Vigne, Senior Criminalist/
Forensic Biologist of the Los Angeles County Sheriff's Dept./
Scientific Services Bureau.

BLACKHEARTED BISCOTTI

2 cups unbleached all-purpose flour
½ tsp. baking soda
½ tsp. double-acting baking powder
1/8 tsp. salt
2 tsp. freshly ground black pepper
½ cup unsalted butter, softened
1 cup sugar
2 large eggs
2 tsp. freshly grated orange zest
1 tsp. freshly grated lemon zest
1 tsp. vanilla
½ tsp. triple sec
1 cup walnuts, toasted lightly and chopped coarse
½ cup pine nuts, toasted lightly

In a bowl sift together flour, baking soda, baking powder, salt, and pepper. Cream butter with sugar until the mixture is light and fluffy, add the eggs, one at a time, beating well after each addition, and beat in the zests, vanilla and triple sec. Stir in the flour mixture, walnuts, and pine nuts, stirring just until a dough is formed; halve the dough. Chill the dough until it can be easily handled.

Working on a large buttered and floured baking sheet, with floured hands form each piece of dough into a flatish log 12 inches long and 2 inches wide and arrange the logs at least 3 inches apart on the sheet. Bake logs on middle rack of oven (preheated to 350°) for 20 to 25 minutes, or until they are pale golden, and let them cool on baking sheet or a rack for 10 minutes. On a cutting board cut logs crosswise on the diagonal into ¾ inch thick slices, arrange biscotti, cut sides down, on a baking sheet and bake at 350° for 7 to 8 minutes on each side, or until pale golden. Transfer biscotti to racks to cool and store in airtight containers where they will keep for several weeks. Makes about 32 biscotti.

> Favorite recipe of Torene Svitil, author of numerous newspaper and magazine articles about film; SinC/LA Board of Directors; "No Crime Unpublished©" Conference Director; short story contributor "Nothing Now Can Ever Come to Any Good" in the SinC/LA anthology, *Murder by Thirteen*.

"Don't mince words—kill him off succinctly."—GTK

"Love is like a mushroom—no roots and deadly poison."—Jean Francis Webb, *No Match for Murder*

"The one mystery we shall never solve is the enigma of human identity."—Emlyn Williams, *Night Must Fall.*

BUTTERBALLS: REST IN PIECES COOKIES
This is an old family recipe from Minnesota
and it's a killer!

1½ cubes butter
1 cup brown sugar
1 large egg
½ tsp. salt
1 tsp. baking powder
1 tsp. vanilla
2 cups flour

Cream ingredients together, adding flour gradually. Roll into balls the size of a large walnut. Roll balls in granulated sugar. Press an almond or piece of walnut into the center of cookie. Bake at 400° for 10 minutes.

Favorite recipe of Anne Riffenburgh, L.C.S.W., author of *Membership News, The Power of Reminiscence,* and *Grandparents and Grandkids: A Celebration of Love,* Huntington Memorial Hospital publications, 1999 and 2000.

Spit and the Pendulum

The development of DNA profiling has multiplied the potential of recovering a suspect's DNA from blood and body fluids to the point where even saliva has become a valued specimen in crime scene analysis. Remarkable laboratory techniques can retrieve DNA from objects that have been licked, chewed, or otherwise nibbled by dastardly doers.

The popularity of gourmet cheese was the downfall in one recent case reported in the forensic literature. A crook was tasting some common Longhorn Jack and apparently not enjoying its flavor, discarded it at the locus of a burglary. A genetic profile was developed from the saliva obtained from the surface of the rejected foodstuff. The unfinished meal brought him to grief and allowed the scales of justice to swing heavily against him. The suspect's DNA signature matched the genetic profile removed from his snack.

Contributed by Michael Bowers, DDS, Forensic Odontologist, forensic writer, lawyer, certified crime scene analyst, and weekend flying instructor.

CHOKE-A-LOT NIBBLERS

3 cups graham cracker crumbs
2 cans sweetened condensed milk
1 6-oz. pkg. chocolate chips
1 stick butter or margarine
1 cup sugar
Wax paper

Soften butter, add graham crackers crumbs. Mix in the sugar. Add the condensed milk while mixing. Then stir in chocolate chips.

Spread onto a greased, waxed-paper-lined pan. (Or you can use foil.) DO NOT USE PLASTIC WRAP, and watch the cooking times! Bake at 350° for about 40 minutes. Invert on a cooling rack, remove the pan, and pull off the waxed paper. Let cool, then cut into oblong bars.

Favorite recipe of C.J. Songer, author of *Bait*, and *Hook*.

Don't Leave Your Jam Thumbprints Cookies

1 cup (2 sticks) butter or margarine
2/3 cup sugar
1 tsp. vanilla
½ tsp. lemon extract
2 large eggs
2½ cups flour
½ tsp. salt
Thick jam, any flavor

Preheat oven to 375°. Grease cookie sheets.

Cream butter and sugar. Blend in vanilla, lemon extract, eggs, flour, and salt. Beat well. Form into 1-inch balls. Place on cookie sheets. Make depression in center of each ball and fill with jam. Pinch together. Bake 13 minutes. Remove from cookie sheet and cool on racks.

Favorite recipe of Mary Terrill, technical writer; past SinC/LA Board of Directors, and editor of the first edition of *Desserticide*.

FATALLY FUDGY BROWNIES

1 cup (2 sticks) butter or margarine
4 1-oz. squares unsweetened chocolate
2 cups sugar
4 large eggs
1 cup flour
1 tsp. vanilla extract
½ tsp. salt (optional)
2 cups nuts, coarsely chopped(optional)

Preheat over to 350°. Grease 9x13-inch cake pan.

In 3-quart saucepan over very low heat, melt butter and chocolate, stirring the mixture constantly. Remove pan from heat and stir the sugar into the chocolate with a spoon. Allow the mixture to cool slightly. Add eggs, one at a time, blending well after each addition. Stir in flour, vanilla, and salt. Add the chopped nuts and stir to blend well.

Pour batter into cake pan, scraping the sides of saucepan with a rubber spatula. Bake 30 to 35 minutes or until a toothpick inserted in center comes out clean. Cool in pan on wire rack. Cut brownies into 24 squares with a sharp knife.

Favorite recipe of Lisa Seidman, TV scriptwriter for "Falcon Crest," "Dallas," "Cagney & Lacey," "Murder, She Wrote," "Knots Landing" and "Sunset Beach." Editor of *Murder by Thirteen* SinC/LA anthology; author of "Over My Shoulder" in the SinC/LA anthology, *A Deadly Dozen.*

Feigning Amnesia to Avoid a Murder Rap

There are two kinds of amnesia: retrograde and anterograde. Retrograde amnesia occurs after a blow to the head or the experience of some shocking event. Memory is lost for the events immediately preceding the injury. Anterograde amnesia occurs when the victim loses all memories after an event and is unable to efficiently form new memories, but otherwise functions naturally.

Murderers are advised to be afflicted by retrograde amnesia in order to utilize the "everything went black and now I can't remember a thing" defense.

Kill 'em with Cookies

1 cup shortening
1 cup sugar
1 large egg
1 cup molasses
4 cups flour
2 tsp. soda
½ tsp. salt
2 tsp. ginger
½ tsp. cinnamon
¼ tsp. cloves

Preheat oven to 350°. Grease cookie sheets.

Thoroughly cream shortening and sugar. Add eggs and mix well. Stir in molasses. Sift together dry ingredients and combine with molasses mixture. Chill thoroughly. Roll into 1-inch diameter balls. Roll balls in sugar, then place 2 inches apart on cookie sheets. Bake 18 to 20 minutes. Remove from sheets and cool on racks.

Favorite recipe of Jeanne Hartman, Voice With A Heart Productions, published author of nonfiction and editor of *Women's Entertainment Network*, SinC/LA Board of Directors 1997-1999.

Interrogation Techniques: The Bluff

This technique may be used to break your alibi and/or prove you are lying about one thing (and therefore may be lying about other, more important things).

For example, if you claim you were at a particular movie at the time the victim died, the investigator might say, "What did you do when the fire alarm sounded?" This is the bluff—there was no fire alarm. You will be watched closely to see if you delay in answering since someone who is lying will not be sure whether the incident occurred or not.

Layer Me In the Grave Dream Bars

¼ cup butter or margarine, soft
½ cup brown sugar, packed
1 cup sifted flour
2 eggs, unbeaten
1 cup brown sugar, packed
1 tsp. vanilla
¼ tsp. salt
1 cup corn flakes
1 cup coconut, shredded
1 cup walnuts, chopped

Preheat oven 350°. Mix first three ingredients, press into 12x8 pan, bake 15 minutes. Mix eggs with 1 cup brown sugar until very light. At low speed, blend the remaining ingredients until just mixed. Spread over baked layer while hot. Bake 20 minutes. Cut into bars while still warm.

Favorite recipe of Sherri L. Board, author of *Angels of Anguish.*

Canadian Flavor of Justice

Police recovered a Canadian beer bottle cap from a crime scene. A tool mark analyst discovered tooth marks on the bottle cap and surmised that the perpetrator had opened the bottle of beer using his teeth. Eventually, when the suspect was arrested, they wanted to obtain a known sample from the suspect for comparison. The suspect refused to deliver a print of his teeth.

A heads-up investigator entered the suspect's jail cell to have a talk. He offered him a bottle of pop and then realized he had "forgotten" to bring a bottle opener. The suspect said, "No problem," and proceeded to bite the top off the soda bottle.

Later, the cop picked up the bottle cap and the tool mark expert proved the same teeth had opened the beer at the crime scene.

Contributed by David Sweet, DMD, Ph.D., Director/Bureau of Legal Dentistry, University of British Columbia

Life Behind Nanaimo Bars

Bottom Layer
½ cup butter
¼ cup granulated sugar
1/3 cup unsweetened cocoa
1 tsp. vanilla
1 egg, beaten
1 cup unsweetened desiccated coconut
2 cups graham cracker crumbs
½ cup chopped walnuts

Filling
¼ cup butter
2 tbsp. milk
2 tbsp. vanilla custard or pudding powder
2 cups sifted icing (confectioners) sugar

Topping
4 ozs. semi-sweet chocolate
1 tbsp. butter

To make the bottom layer, melt butter in a saucepan over low heat. Add the sugar, cocoa, vanilla and egg. Cook, stirring, over medium heat until the mixture thickens. Remove from heat and stir in the coconut, crumbs and walnuts. Pat firmly into a buttered 9-inch square pan. Refrigerate for at least one hour.

To make the filling, cream the butter. Beat in the milk, custard powder and icing sugar. If the mixture is too thick to spread, add a few more drops of milk. Spread over the bottom layer and refrigerate for 30 minutes, or until firm.

For the top layer, melt the chocolate and butter and blend together. Spread over the filling.

Before the chocolate hardens completely, cut into squares. Refrigerate for at least one hour. Makes about 24 squares.

Nanaimo Bars were, so the story goes, concocted to disguise illicit booze run from Canada to the USA during Prohibition. (We're a rascally bunch, you see.) Whatever the real story behind this divine creation, it's an all-time favorite.

Favorite recipe of Taylor Smith, author *of The Best of Enemies, Random Acts, The Innocents Club* and more.

Also the favorite recipe of Larry Hill, contributing author in SinC/LA anthology, *Murder by Thirteen*, past member of the Board of Directors, and musician.

MACABRE POISON BALLS

1 cup butter
¾ cup confectioner's sugar
2 cups flour
1 tsp. vanilla
1 cup chopped pecans or walnuts

Preheat oven at 350°.

Mix all ingredients; roll by hand into a small ¾-inch ball then roll into a small bowl of extra fine confectioner's sugar. Place on a baking sheet. Bake at 350° for 30 minutes. Roll again in the confectioner's sugar while hot. Then place on a cooling rack. When cool put in airtight container. Makes 3 dozen.

Favorite recipe of Diane Jay Bouchard, author of nonfiction magazine and newspaper articles, and editor of *Desserticide II, aka Just Desserts and Deathly Advice.* SinC/LA Vice President 1995-1997 and President 1997-2002.

Justice Must Wait For the Hungry Crime Fighter

Nothing escapes the determined crime fighter's physical evidence connected to a crime. The evidence technician working a homicide case considered the kitchen a prime target for investigation. Perseverance paid off, when a half-eaten chocolate cookie was seen and thought to be significant to the case.

After all the proper documentation, collection and transportation was performed, the item was in its proper place in the crime lab refrigerator. High tech forensic investigation progressed nicely and the suspect cookie was retained for display at the trial.

Unfortunately, the evidence was returned to a different refrigerator, this one located in the lunchroom. The effort to reclaim the cookie was frustrated when it was eaten by an overly enthusiastic criminalist.

Contributed by Michael Bowers, DDS, Forensic Odontologist, forensic writer, lawyer, certified crime scene analyst and a weekend flying instructor.

MANSLAUGHTER MINT BROWNIES

4 1-oz. chocolate sqares (bitter, semi, or unsweetened)
¾ cup butter
1 heaping tsp. instant coffee
4 large eggs
2 cups sugar
1 tbsp. vanilla
1 cup flour
2 cups mint chocolate chips
1 cup walnuts or pecans, chopped
Powdered sugar (optional)

Preheat oven to 425°. Grease a 9x13-inch cake pan.

Melt chocolate, butter, and instant coffee using a micro-wave oven or double-boiler. Stir and allow to cool to room temperature. In a small mixer bowl, beat eggs and sugar until creamy. In a large mixer bowl, combine cooled chocolate mixture and egg-sugar mixture. Beat well. Add vanilla. Add flour, about ¼ cup at a time, beating after each addition. Stir in mint chocolate chips and nuts. Turn batter into the cake pan.

Bake about 20 minutes until top has a crust and brownies pull away from the sides of the pan. Sprinkle with powdered sugar, if desired. These brownies always seem better the second day if they last that long!

Variations: Substitute butterscotch chips, toffee chips, or chocolate raspberry chips (made by Hershey and often hard to find but well worth the effort) for the mint chocolate chips.

Favorite recipe of Jamie Wallace, contributing author "Driven to Kill" in the SinC/LA anthology, *A Deadly Dozen*. Board member in '96 and Vice President '97-'99, and Conference Director, "No Crime Unpublished©."

"Time is a greater murderer than any man or woman. Time is the murderer that gets caught."—William Irish, *Phantom Lady*

"It's not taking on death that's tough, it's taking off life."—Cornell Woolrich, "One Night in Barcelona."

"Crime doesn't pay enough."—DJB

NIGHTSHADE NIGHTY-NIGHTS

Do not make these cookies in rainy weather. The meringue won't hold up just like a bank robbery gone arwy.

5 egg whites
¼ tsp. salt
1 cup sugar
1 cup semi-sweet chocolate chips OR mint chips
1-2 drops of food coloring for holidays (optional)
3 clean brown grocery bags or parchment sheets.

Beat egg whites with salt (and food coloring) until soft peaks form. Gradually beat in sugar; continue to beat until stiff peaks form. Fold in chocolate chips gently. Place one large tablespoon of mixture in several spots on a shopping bag (with no ink advertisements on the paper side you use) or parchment paper.

Place in a preheated oven at 450 degrees and say "nighty-night." *Turn off the oven.* Let stand overnight or at least 5 hours. Carefully remove cookies from the paper. Store in an airtight container.

Small pesky children especially love to makes these cookies. Makes about 25 cookies.

Favorite recipe of Diane Jay Bouchard, author of nonfiction magazine and newspaper articles and editor of *Desserticide II aka Just Desserts and Deathly Advice*; Board of Directors: Vice President 1995-1997 and President 1997-2002.

Beating Lie Detectors

Generally speaking, the results of a polygraph examination are not admissible in a court of law, but investigators may use them to ascertain what you may be lying about.

Your pulse rate and breathing patterns are monitored and appear as a series of graphs. The concept behind the lie detector is that tension created by telling a lie will be reflected in rises in blood pressure, breathing rate, and sweat production. Investigators will ask you a series of innocuous questions to establish a "base" response, then watch your responses to incriminating questions.

How to beat the system? On random questions, tighten your muscles (to raise blood pressure) and breathe more rapidly as you answer. With a little forethought you will ensure that your responses are too confusing to be of use!

Pernicious Peanut Butter Cookies

¼ cup shortening
¼ cup butter
½ cup chunky peanut butter
½ cup granulated sugar
1 large egg
1¼ cup flour
¾ tsp. baking soda
½ tsp. baking powder
¼ tsp. salt
½ cup brown sugar

Preheat oven to 375°. Lightly grease cookie sheets.

Mix thoroughly butter, shortening, peanut butter, granulated sugar, brown sugar, and egg. Blend in flour, soda, baking powder, and salt. Cover and chill. Shape chilled dough into 1-inch balls. Place balls 3 inches apart on cookie sheet. Using a fork dipped in flour, flatten balls to 2-inch rounds, making a criss-cross pattern with the tines. Bake 10 to 12 minutes or until set but not hard. Cool on racks.

Death Row Modification: Substitute ¼ cup butter for the shortening.

Favorite recipe of Larry Hill, contributing author in SinC/LA anthology *Murder by Thirteen*, past member of the Board of Directors, and musician.

Death by Julia

No less a chef
than Julia Child
says if you want
to drive 'em wild
with pies and cookies,
tarts and cakes,
a heap of butter
is all it takes!
—by Anne Riffenburgh

[Anne's thought is that too much butter will clog the victim's arteries a tad and finish him/her off faster. However, Julia child is 90 and has followed her own advice religiously. Must be the red wine ... —The Editors]

"To die will be an awfully big adventure."—
James M. Barrie, *Peter Pan*

"Hammer home the point—on his head."—
GTK

PHARAOH'S CURSE KONAFA

1 pound konafa* pastry (found in Middle Eastern markets)
1 cup (2 sticks) butter, melted and cooled
Cream Filling (recipe follows)
Syrup (recipe follows)

*Pronounced ko-NAH-fa. The raw dough looks like unbaked shredded wheat, but it is actually phyllo "spaghetti" rather than sheets.

Preheat oven to 350°. Grease a 9x13-inch cake pan.

Place the konafa pastry in a large bowl. With your fingers, carefully pull out and separate the strands as much as possible so they no longer stick together too much. Pour melted butter over the loosened mass. Work it in thoroughly with your fingers, pulling and mixing so each strand is entirely coated with butter. Put half the pastry into the cake pan. Spread Cream Filling evenly over pastry. Cover the filling with the rest of the pastry, evening it out and flattening it with the palm of your hand.

Bake 35 to 45 minutes at 350°, then raise oven temperature to 450° for 10 to 15 minutes longer until the pastry is a light golden color. Remove from oven and pour half the cold Syrup over the hot konafa. Wait 10 minutes; pour remaining Syrup over the konafa. Let stand 1-8 hours. Cut in 2-inch squares or diamond shapes to serve.

Cream Filling
4 tbsp. rice flour (or grind rice in blender until it's flour.)
2 tbsp. sugar
2½ cups milk
½ cup heavy cream

Mix rice flour and sugar with ½ cup milk until it is a

smooth paste. Boil the rest of the milk and add the rice paste slowly, stirring vigorously. Simmer while stirring, until mixture is very thick. Allow to cool. Add heavy cream, and mix well.

SYRUP*
1 ¼ cups sugar
½ cup water
1 tbsp. lemon juice
1 tbsp. orange blossom water

Stir sugar, water, and lemon juice over moderate heat. Simmer until it thickens and coats the spoon. Stir in orange blossom water and cook for 2 minutes more. Cool completely.

*You might try 1½ times the syrup. You want this dessert very moist, but not swimming in syrup.

> Favorite recipe of Susan M. Stephenson, author of "How to Grow Orchids Outdoors in Southern California," in the *American Orchid Society Bulletin,* and other articles about orchids, and public relations materials; Board of Directors, 1995-2002 as secretary, membership chair; *Ransome Notes* editor; and *Murder by Thirteen* anthology committee member and PBS Pledge Drive Coordinator.

RUN FOR YOUR LIFE CHERRY SLIMS
If you've been dying for a low calorie cookie, this one will
finish you off.

½ cup non-fat egg substitute (or two eggs)
1 cup dark brown sugar, packed
½ cup white sugar
2 tbsp. non-fat milk
1 tbsp. butter or margarine, softened
1 tsp. vanilla extract
1½ cups rolled oats
1 cup all-purpose flour
1 tsp. baking soda
1 tsp. salt
1½ cups dried cherries (or cranberries)
(If you're living dangerously, and don't care about calories,
add 1 cup chopped pecans)

Combine egg substitute, brown sugar, white sugar, non-fat milk, butter and vanilla.

Grind 1¼ cups rolled oats in food processor or blender to consistency of flour, and combine with all-purpose flour, baking soda and salt. Stir into sugar/egg mixture. Stir in remaining ¼ cup rolled oats and cherries. Drop onto greased baking sheets by tablespoon.

Bake at 375° about eight minutes, or until center tests done. Remove from baking sheets to wire racks while still warm. Makes about three dozen cookies.

Favorite recipe of Esta Sullivan, former technical writer, member of SinC/LA nominating committee and has just completed writing her first novel.

"Dead men tell no lies."—DJB

"The one mystery we shall never solve is the enigma of human identity."—Emlyn Williams

"Murder in haste, repent in pen stripes."
                                    —DJB

SATURDAY NIGHT SPECIALS
These chewy, delicious, no-fat cookies, are real killers,
Saturday night or any other night.

2 cups 10X (confectioner's) sugar
¾ cup all-purpose flour
½ tsp. baking powder
½ cup egg whites (4 large eggs)
½ cup chopped dried fruit, (raisins, dates, apples, and/or cherries.)
¼ cup pecans, chopped

Preheat oven to 325°. Coat cookie sheets with nonstick vegetable cooking spray.

Combine sugar, flour, baking powder and egg whites in large mixing bowl. Mix with electric mixer until well blended. Stir in dried fruit and pecans.

Drop batter by slightly rounded teaspoons onto prepared cookie sheets, leaving 4 inches between cookies.

Bake for 12-15 minutes or until lightly browned. Remove cookies immediately with spatula to wire racks to cool.

Makes about 4 dozen cookies.

Note: These cookies may be molded into rounded shape by pressing over rolling pin or drinking glass until they have cooled.

Favorite recipe of Esta Sullivan, former technical writer, member of SinC/LA nominating committee and has just completed writing her first novel.

Disposing of the Body: General Pointers

There are two principal reasons for disposing of the body:

1) Short-term: to conceal the crime long enough for you to either escape or concoct a suitable alibi.

2) Long-term: to ensure that your victim is never found and identified.

A cautionary note: Be aware that even if your victim's body is disposed of so effectively that it is never found, this does not guarantee your safety. It doesn't seem quite fair, but murder charges can be pursued and a conviction obtained, even if the body is missing.

SERIOUS HARD TIME ORANGE CARROT COOKIES

1 cup shortening
¾ cup sugar
1 cup cooked mashed carrots
1-2 eggs
1 tsp. vanilla
2 cup flour
2 tsp. baking powder
½ tsp. salt
¾ cup coconut flakes. (optional)

Cream shortening and sugar until fluffy. Add carrots, egg and vanilla; mix well. Stir in the dry ingredients which have been sifted together. Drop batter by teaspoonful 2 inches apart on greased baking sheet. Bake at 350° for 10-20 minutes. While warm, frost with Golden Glow frosting.

GOLDEN GLOW FROSTING
1 tbsp. butter or margarine
1 cup sifted powdered sugar.
Juice of ½ orange
Grated rind of 1 orange

Combine all ingredients; mix well. Spread over cookies. Yield 4-5 dozen.

Favorite recipe of Bonnie and Clyde: "We'd rob a bank for this recipe—just give us a chance."

Arsenic: The King of Poisons

A metallic poison naturally occurring in lead and iron ore, used widely since ancient times, and known as "the king of poisons." Arsenic is a white, tasteless powder that resembles powdered sugar or flour. Arsenic has one other helpful quality—it is cumulative, so many small doses can be given over time. Be aware, however, that tolerance builds up. See Dorothy Sayers' *Strong Poison*, which utilized this fact in the plot.

Another reason that poisoners have been so keen to use arsenic is that the symptoms mimic ordinary illnesses, such as food poisoning.

Poisoners using arsenic are advised to encourage cremation of their victims, as arsenic remains in the body, which can lead to an accurate estimation of when administration of the poison began.

Sweet Revenge Chocolate Bars

This yummy confection could easily disguise a bitter white poison sprinkled on top along with the powdered sugar.

1 cup + 2 tbsp. flour
1½ cups brown sugar
½ cup (1 stick) butter or margarine
½ tsp. baking powder
1 tsp. vanilla
¼ tsp. salt
1 12-oz. pkg. semi-sweet chocolate chips
2 large eggs, beaten
Powdered sugar and ???

Preheat oven to 350°. Butter a 9x13-inch cake pan.

Sift together 1 cup flour and ½ cup brown sugar. Cut in the butter or margarine until the mixture has pie crust consistency. Pat the mixture in the bottom of cake pan. Bake until slightly brown. While this crust is baking, combine the remaining 1 cup brown sugar and 2 tablespoons flour. Add baking powder, vanilla, salt, chocolate chips, and eggs. Mix well. Spread evenly on baked crust and continue baking for 20 minutes. Cool. Sprinkle with powdered sugar. Cut into bars.

Favorite recipe of Judith K. Smith, author of a short story in SinC/LA anthology, *Murder by Thirteen*, past Board of Directors member; "No Crime Unpublished©" Conference Director; and is currently writing a Bea Silver Mystery.

Perseverance Pays Off

Usually Forensic Toxicology is routine; however, some-times a case comes along that is anything but routine. From PCP in rice pudding to pine oil cleanser in pasta, many of these cases pose a challenge to the analyst to devise new methods of detection.

One such case involves the use of GHB (gamma hydroxy butyrate) in Goldschlager liquor. It was alleged that two men were drugging women with GHB, and untoward activities occurred.

When one of the victims complained, police searched the defendant's residence and found liquor, Margarita salt, and several Internet articles on GHB. The laboratory ana-lyzed the evidence and determined that there was GHB in the Margarita salt. The Goldschlager liquor was most likely used to disguise the taste of GHB. Both defendants were later convicted of poisoning and other charges. So if it tastes weird—don't drink it.

Contributed by Susan Perez, Criminalistic Laboratory Tech-nician/Forensic Toxicology Los Angeles County Sheriff's Dept. /Scientific Services Bureau.

COLD KILLER COMPOTE

Slice and dice to good effect: 1 large can each pears, peaches, chunk pineapple, mandarin oranges, cherry pie filling

Drain the pears, peaches, pineapple, and oranges in a colander for 4 hours. Preheat oven to 325°. Quarter the pears and peaches—an excellent opportunity to sharpen your slicing skills—then mix together with the pineapple and oranges. Place in a 2-quart, oven-proof glass bowl. Pour the cherry pie filling over the top. Do not stir in the pie filling. Bake 1 hour.

This hot variation of a cold favorite can also be served as a side dish—in case you don't want your guests hanging around for dessert.

Favorite recipe of Sandy Siegal, author of daytime and prime-time TV episodes, short stories, magazine and newspaper articles, and contributor to the SinC/LA anthology, *Murder by Thirteen*. Past member of the Board of Directors

Manslaughter

Manslaughter is distinguished from murder as being the unlawful (but unintentional) killing of a human being without malice.

Voluntary manslaughter occurs when the killing results from "a sudden quarrel or the heat of passion."

Involuntary manslaughter has two divisions. First, killing "in the commission of an unlawful act, not amounting to a felony." Second—suitable for those using *Desserticide II*—killing someone because of the lack of due caution.

If you feign confusion over the dessert ingredients, you may be charged with involuntary manslaughter rather than murder.

MALICE AFORETHOUGHT BAKED APPLES

6 large Golden Delicious apples
¼ cup brown sugar
1 tbsp. cinnamon
¼ cup walnuts, chopped
¼ cup raisins
2 tbsp. butter

Preheat oven to 375°.

Wash and partially core the apples, leaving ½-inch at the base. Place the apples in a baking pan. Combine brown sugar, cinnamon, walnuts, and raisins. Fill the apples with this mixture. Dot with butter.

Pour ½-inch water into the bottom of the pan. Bake 45 minutes. Cool. Baste apples with the pan juices before serving.

Favorite recipe of Mae Woods, television producer of *When Danger Follows You Home*, screenwriter for *Tales of the Crypt*, editor of *Murder by Thirteen* SinC/LA anthology and a SinC/LA Board of Directors member.

Justice Really Does Prevail

On a cold and rainy night, during a double homicide investigation, a man had been found along the side of the freeway, outside his locked car with near-fatal stab wounds. He was transported to the nearest hospital. When the highway patrol looked over the side of the freeway where the man was found, the officers discovered many items that related to the murders that had occurred earlier.

After examination of the vehicle, it was determined that the person had locked his keys in the car while getting rid of the evidence. Otherwise the authorities would not have had a clue, nor found the items of evidence which included ... the murder weapon.

Contributed by Beverly A. Kerr, Senior Criminalist of the Los Angeles County Sheriff's Dept/Scientific Services Bureau.

SANGUINARY PURSUITS FRUIT SALAD
Boysenberries will be boysenberries.

1 pkg. raspberry gelatin
1 cup boiling water
1 cup unsweetened applesauce
1 cup stewed or frozen boysenberries
Whipped cream (optional)

Dissolve the gelatin in boiling water. Cool until syrupy. Stir in remaining ingredients and chill until thick. If you can't find boysenberries, you can substitute frozen, unsweetened raspberries, although this will make the dessert less "boysenous." You may increase its lethality by serving it with whipped cream.

If this dish is served at a Midwest potluck, be sure to get your share early because any kind of gelatin dessert (particularly if it includes marshmallows) is considered salad, and this one is too good to miss.

> Favorite recipe of Rose Felsenburg Kaplan, author of stories, nonfiction and poetry; and winner of "The 1998 California Social Worker of the Year."

Alcohol

An extremely slow way to kill someone, but much fun can be had by all. Note that alcohol leads to a reduction in coordination, vision, memory, reasoning abilities, and judgment.

You might consider using alcohol in conjunction with a more rapid method of dispatch.

"My favorite desserts are the whipped ones."—Marquis de Sade

Violent Rummed Bananas
Follow your taste buds as to amounts.

2-4 ripe bananas
Splash Myers' rum
2 tbsp. brown sugar
2 tbsp. butter or margarine

Melt butter in a sauté pan over medium-high heat. Slice bananas into the pan and let them cook until mushy. Add brown sugar—a couple of tablespoons, more if you have a sweet tooth. Stir, coating the bananas. Add a splash of rum—more if you like, but don't flood the pan. When dessert is bubbling, use a long fireplace match to flame the rum. Dessert is ready when nice and mushy.

This dessert is great by itself, but really terrific over ice cream (especially vanilla or coffee) or sponge cake.

Favorite recipe of Jamie Wallace, contributing author, "Driven to Kill" in the SinC/LA anthology, *A Deadly Dozen*. Board of Directors, 1996 and Vice President 1997-1999 and Conference Director for 1999 "No Crime Unpublished©."

Recipe For A Frame

The best way to implicate someone for murder is to plant physical evidence from the person on the victim.

A good way to get physical evidence from the would-be suspect is while he is in the hospital, preferably unconscious. First, pull out a few hairs. As you know, the roots of hairs that fall out are different from those that are pulled out. Pick a few hairs from the pillow, too.

If possible, take a vial of blood.

At the murder scene, put the pulled-out hairs in the victims' hand and drop the fallen-out ones around the body. Smash a few lamps.

Liberally sprinkle the drops of blood nearby.

Be sure that the would-be suspect does not have an alibi, but make sure you do!

Contributed by Anne Riffenburgh, L.C.S.W., author of *Membership News, The Power of Reminiscence,* and *Grandparents and Grandkids: A Celebration of Love,* Huntington Memorial Hospital publications, 1999 and 2000.

MANIACAL MOUSSE

1 envelope unflavored gelatin
1 tbsp. sugar
½ cup milk
1 6-oz.pkg. semi-sweet chocolate chips
1 tsp. vanilla extract
1½ cups Cool Whip® or whipped cream

In medium saucepan, mix unflavored gelatin with sugar. Blend in milk. Let stand 1 minute. Stir over low heat until gelatin is completely dissolved, about 5 minutes. Add chocolate and continue cooking, stirring constantly, until chocolate is melted. With wire whisk beat mixture until chocolate is blended. Stir in vanilla. Pour into large bowl and chill, stirring occasionally until mixture mounds slightly when dropped from spoon. Fold in whipped topping. Turn into 6 dessert dishes; chill until set. Garnish with additional topping.

> Favorite recipe of Lisa Seidman, TV scriptwriter for "Falcon Crest," "Dallas," "Cagney & Lacey," "Murder, She Wrote," "Knots Landing," and "Sunset Beach." Editor of SinC/LA anthology *Murder by Thirteen,* author of "Sunset Over My Shoulder" in the SinC/LA anthology, *A Deadly Dozen.*

Dying Declarations from Not-Quite-Dead Victims

If you are unfortunate enough to have a victim refuse to die, do try to discourage his or her declaration to a third party, particularly a police officer. Although such a declaration is hearsay evidence, it will be given special weight by the authorities and may be used at your trial.

Conditions for a dying declaration: 1. The victim must believe that he or she is definitely about to depart this life (You should vigorously assure your victim that this is not the case!). 2. The victim must explain how he or she came to his/her present condition (Announce that the victim is confused or mistaken.). 3. The victim must die (a sigh of relief from you!).

Ax Murderer's Apple Apricot Pie
A Lizzie Borden Specialty

1/3 cup granulated sugar
1/3 cup brown sugar
3 tbsp. all-purpose flour
¼ tsp. salt
¼ tsp. ground cinnamon
1 can (1 lb. 14-oz.) apricots, halved and drained
1 tbsp. lemon juice
1 can (1 lb. 4-oz.) pie-sliced apples, not drained
1 tbsp. butter or margarine
Pastry for 2 pie crusts

Combine sugars, salt, flour, and cinnamon; stir into apples in a mixing bowl. Add lemon juice and mix well. Cut apricot halves in half; fold into apple mixture. Line 9" pie pan with the pastry; add fruit mixture. Dot with bits of butter or margarine. Adjust top crust, cutting slits for the escape of steam; seal and flute edges. Sprinkle top with additional granulated sugar. Bake in hot oven 400° for 40 minutes, or until crust is golden brown.

Favorite recipe of Linda Bivens, owner of Crime Time Books Bookstore; a great mystery buff, SinC/LA member and a lady who knows where all the bodies are buried.

Effective Lying

The ability to lie effectively is of inestimable value to someone guilty of desserticide.

The verbal and non-verbal cues that indicate someone is lying include nervous mannerisms (licking lips), hesitating before answering questions, giving brief replies, avoiding eye contact, and shifting posture frequently.

Practice your lying. When interrogated, keep your hands still, even though tempted to fiddle with something. Do not stare fixedly at the investigator, but meet his or her glance in a natural manner. Do not make vague, sweeping statements, but reply to questions with factual answers. If you sense that a question may trap you, frown and say something like, "I'm sorry, I can't quite remember …"

DEAD IN THE GRAVE BROWN BETTY PIE

10-12 apples
Cinnamon to taste
½ cup white sugar
1½ cups flour
2 cups brown sugar, packed
1 cup butter or margarine, softened

Peel apples and cut into slices and put into a deep buttered baking dish. (I use a 9x14x2 glass dish.) Sprinkle lavishly with the white sugar and cinnamon. In a separate dish, blend the flour, brown sugar and softened butter or margarine with a fork. Pack the flour mix firmly over the apple mixture.

Bake at 350° until apples are tender and the crust is firm (approximately 30-45 minutes,)

Favorite recipe of C.J. Songer, author of *Bait*, and *Hook*.

"Some poison'd by their wives ..."
            —Shakespeare: *Richard II*, Act III

"In the extreme instances of reaction against
convention, female murderers get sheaves of
offers of marriage."—George Bernard Shaw,
Preface to *Getting Married*

HELLUVA HOMICIDAL HONEY CHEESE PIE

Crust and Topping
1/3 cup butter
¼ cup honey
3 tbsp. brown sugar, packed
3 cups natural cereal (crushed coarsely)

Combine butter, honey and brown sugar in medium sauce pan. Cook over low heat, stirring occasionally, until butter melts and sugar dissolves. Stir in cereal. Mix well. Reserve ¼ cup cereal mixture for topping. Press remaining cereal mixture firmly onto bottom and sides of lightly oiled 10-inch pie pan.

Filling
¼ cup water
1 8-oz. block of cream cheese, softened
½ cup honey
1/8 tsp. salt
1 8-oz. carton unflavored yogurt
1 envelope + 2 tsp. unflavored gelatin
2 cups heavy cream, whipped
2 tbsp. lemon juice

Soften gelatin in combined water and lemon juice. Stir over low heat until dissolved. Beat together cream cheese, honey, and salt until well blended. Gradually add yogurt and dissolved gelatin mixture. Mix until well blended. Chill about 5 minutes. Fold in whipped cream, then spoon into crust. Sprinkle with reserved ¼ cup cereal mixture. Chill until firm and serve.

Favorite recipe of Gayle Pfaucht, editor of SinC/LA newsletter *Ransom Notes*, Board of Directors 1998-2002. Gayle is currently writing a mystery series.

"Nobody ever commits a crime without doing something stupid."—Oscar Wilde

"When a person tampers with the truth there
is always some unexpected little detail to trip
him up."—D.M. Devine, *My Brother's Killer*

"Jealousy is worse than liquor. It biteth like
the adder."—Cleve F. Adams, *Up Jumped the
Devil*

POISON PUCKER RHUBARB PIE

1 pie crust, ready made
2 eggs
1 cup sour cream
1½ cups sugar
2 tbsp. flour
1 tsp. vanilla
¼ tsp. salt
3 cups chopped rhubarb
Streusel Topping (recipe below)

Mix eggs and sour cream; stir in sugar and flour. Add vanilla, salt and rhubarb. Pile into pie crust, cover with foil and bake for 15 minutes at 400°. Reduce heat to 350° and bake for 20 minutes. Sprinkle on Streusel Topping and bake uncovered for 25 minutes more or until set.

STREUSEL TOPPING
¼ cup brown sugar
¼ cup flour
3 tbsp. butter

Mix ingredients together and sprinkle as directed.

Favorite recipe of Dorothy Rellas, author of novel, *Hidden Motives*, "Round Midnight" in the SinC/LA anthology, *A Deadly Dozen*, short story for *Future* Magazine, and "Let's Get to the Skinny." Board of Directors and treasurer of SinC/LA 1997-2002.

Aconitine

A vegetable alkaloid poison derived from *Aconitum napellus*, the wolfsbane or monkshood plant. The leaf looks like parsley and the root like horseradish. Its bitter taste must be disguised—a sweet confection will do the trick!

In solution, it can be absorbed through the skin and was greatly favored in ancient Greece and Rome as a means of removing inconvenient people, particularly politicians.

Poisonous Pavlova Passion Pie

5 egg whites
¼ tsp. salt
1 cup sugar
Assorted fresh fruit, ice cream, lemon curd, drizzled chocolate with chopped nuts for topping.

Beat egg whites with salt until soft peaks form. Gradually beat in sugar; continue to beat until stiff peaks form.
Spread mixture in a well greased 8x8x- inch pan. Place in
an oven preheated to 450° and close door. *Turn off the heat.*
Let stand overnight or 5 hours before removing from
oven. Cut and top with fresh chopped fruit, ice cream,
whipped cream and minced nuts. Yields 4-6 servings.

Favorite recipe of Lucrezia Borgia: "My kind
of recipe."

"Never tick off your editor, publisher, or the
IRS—any one of them can do you in as an
author."—DJB

So Many Reasons to Commit Arson and So Little Time

Two men were carrying on a feud, which for one party escalated to a desire for violence.

The angry one found such services for-hire in a high-crime city neighborhood for a fee of $1000. The hired crook sublet the job to someone dumber and cheaper for $75 and then drove him to the victim's suburban apartment.

Armed with a gallon of gasoline, Dumber looked for the victim's car but it was locked in the garage. He then knocked on the apartment door. Mr. Suburb talked to him through the door without opening it.

In a hurry to dispatch his $75 job, the perpetrator threw gasoline on the door and lit a match. The burning door attracted the neighbor's attention as did Dumber putting out the fire on his pants while escaping. He tripped over a speed bump and fell. His driver, the first hired crook, was of course long gone. Dumber was later arrested, complete with torn pants, skinned knees, gasoline-soaked clothes, and speed bump marks on the toes of his shoes.

Contributed by Vickie L. Clawson, Senior Criminalist/Physical Evidence Section/Scientific Services of the Los Angeles Sheriff's Dept.

BANEFUL BREAD AND BUTTER PUDDING WITH LAST GASP SAUCE

8 slices French bread
3 tbsp. butter or margarine
1/3 cup light brown sugar, packed
1 tsp. cinnamon
1/3 cup walnuts, chopped
1/3 cup semi-sweet chocolate chips
3 large eggs, slightly beaten
1/3 cup granulated sugar
½ tsp. vanilla
Dash salt
2¼ cups milk, scalded
¼ cup Irish Cream liqueur
Last Gasp Sauce (recipe below)

Heat oven to 350°. Butter a 1½ quart casserole.

Toast bread slices slightly and spread butter on one side of each. Sprinkle with brown sugar, cinnamon, chopped nuts, and chocolate chips. Press slices of bread together, forming four sandwiches. Cut off crusts, then cut into rectangular strips. Arrange strips in casserole. Blend eggs, granulated sugar, salt, vanilla, and liqueur. Gradually stir in scalded milk. Pour mixture over bread. Place casserole in a pan of very hot water (1-inch deep) and bake 65 to 70 minutes or until a knife inserted in the center comes out clean. Serve pudding warm or cold with Last Gasp Sauce.

LAST GASP SAUCE
6 tbsp. butter
½ cup granulated sugar
1 large egg
Irish Cream liqueur to taste

Cream butter and sugar. Cook in a double-boiler until sugar is well dissolved. Partially cool and add beaten egg. Whip quickly so egg does not curdle. Cool and add liqueur to taste. Whip before serving and pour over pudding.

Favorite recipe of Kris Neri, author of sixty short stories, and mystery novel, *Revenge of the Gypsy Queen*, Derringer Award winner for "L.A. Justice" in SinC/LA anthology *Murder by Thirteen*, and "Sentence imposed" *in A Deadly Dozen;* SinC/LA Vice President 1994-1995 and President 1995-1997.

DEAD MAN'S FLAN DE FIESTA

1¾ cups sugar
3 egg whites
8 egg yolks
2¾ cans evaporated milk
2 tsp. vanilla extract

Put one cup of sugar into a heavy pan and place over a low flame, stirring constantly until it turns a deep golden brown. Remove instantly and pour into mold in which the flan will be baked. Tip the mold around until all sides are coated with caramel. Let cool while making the custard.

Beat egg whites and yolks together with a fork or wire whisk until lemon-colored. Add remaining sugar, milk, and vanilla. Strain into the coated mold. Cover with foil and place in a pan of boiling water that reaches more than halfway up the outside of the mold. Bake at 350° for an hour or more. Test the doneness by inserting a broom straw or a silver knife. If it comes out clean, refrigerate flan until serving. Bring flan to room temperature and unmold. Or it can be served from the mold.

Favorite recipe of Helene Juarez Phipps, author of *Authentic Mexican Cooking*; columnist for *Latina Style* Magazine; Mystery Writers of America anthology, "Copcade" and numerous other works.

"There is no person who is not dangerous for someone."—Marie de Sevigne, in a letter

"It's for your own good—if you kill him good."—GTK

"It is a sin to believe evil of others, but it is seldom a mistake."—H.L Mencken, *A Mencken Chrestomathy*

"To protect and serve, forgive and forget."— *Cops & Robbers, DJB*

DEATH WARRANT RAISIN RICE PUDDING

½ cup rice uncooked
1 qt. milk
½ cup seedless raisins
1/3 cup margarine
3 eggs, beaten
½ cup sugar
1 tsp. vanilla
¼ tsp. salt
Cinnamon or nutmeg to taste

Mix rice with 2 cups milk in top of double-boiler; cook over hot water until rice is tender. Add raisins and margarine. Combine eggs, sugar, vanilla, salt and remaining milk. Stir into the hot rice mixture. Pour into a greased 1½ qt. baking dish. Sprinkle cinnamon or nutmeg. Set in a baking pan filled half with warm water. Bake at 325° for 30 minutes until set. Serves 6.

Favorite recipe of Barry A.J. Fisher, author of *Techniques of Crime Scene Investigation*, 6th edition; Director of the Scientific Services Bureau, Los Angeles County Sheriff's Dept., President of the International Association of Forensic Scientists '96-'99.

Thallium

Discovered in 1861 by Sir William Crookes, thallium is a heavy metal similar to lead. For the professional poisoner, thallium has several worthwhile properties; it dissolves in water, is almost tasteless, and its initial symptoms mimic the aches and pains of the flu.

Thallium has the convenience of being a cumulative poison, so it can be administered over a period of time. It does have one drawback—it causes loss of hair. If you feel tingling or numbness in extremities and noticeable hair loss, you would be advised to look at your nearest and dearest.

Don't Trifle with Me!

A traditional British poisoner's delight.

1-2 packages jelly rolls
1 large can fruit cocktail or sliced peaches
2 tbsp. Harvey's Bristol Cream sherry
Vanilla Custard (recipe below)
Whipped cream (optional)

Slice jelly rolls into 1-inch slices. Line the bottom of a deep dish with the slices. Sprinkle with sherry and let stand for 10 minutes. Drain the canned fruit and spoon over jelly roll. Top with Vanilla Custard. Refrigerate. Garnish with whipped cream if desired.

Vanilla Custard
¾ cup sugar
2 tbsp. cornstarch
1/8 tsp. salt
2 cups half & half
4 large egg yolks, well beaten
2 tbsp. butter
1½ tsp. vanilla
1 cup heavy cream, whipped

Combine sugar, cornstarch, and salt in the top of a double-boiler. Over medium heat, gradually stir in half & half. Cover and cook for 8 minutes without stirring. Uncover and cook another 10 minutes, stirring frequently. Stir in butter, egg yolks, and vanilla. Remove from heat and cool 5 minutes. Fold in whipped cream.

Favorite recipe of Mae Woods, television producer of *When Danger Follows You Home*, screenwriter for *Tales from the Crypt*, editor of SinC/LA anthology, *Murder by Thirteen*, member of SinC/LA Board of Directors.

"Never carry a loaded gun in your pants pocket ... as it can have repercussions."—DJB

"Murder is a serious business. The slightest slip may be disastrous."—Frances Iles, (aka Anthony Berkeley Cox), *Malice Aforethought*

"A criminal is only as clever as his ego allows."—DJB

HAND OVER YOUR BREAD PUDDING

1 cup mandarin oranges
Grand Marnier, to cover
1 lb. egg bread, broken into 1-2 inch cubes, poppy seeds
included
1 tbsp. orange extract
Custard Sauce
Topping

Drain orange slices, pat dry; and marinate overnight or longer. Before using, pat dry again; and reserve marinade.

CUSTARD SAUCE
1 qt. half & half
8 eggs
8 egg yolks
1¼ cup sugar
1½ cups orange juice (preferably fresh)
½ cup Grand Marnier marinade
2 tsp. nutmeg /or 1 tbsp. cinnamon

Heat cream. Beat eggs, yolks and sugar slowly, and pour in heated cream and mix well. Add juice and Grand Marnier (and nutmeg/cinnamon if desired). Blend well. Set aside 2 cups for topping.

TOPPING
2 tsp. cornstarch
2 cups Custard Sauce
2 tsp. vanilla (or almond or coconut extract)
Milk or Grand Marnier to thin.

Mix cornstarch with Custard Sauce; cook slowly on low until temperature reaches 165°. Cool. Add vanilla. If sauce needs thinning, add milk or Grand Marnier.

Construction:

Butter a bundt mold. Add orange slices and extract to Custard Sauce; pour into pan alternately with bread. Let the custard soak in.

Set mold in a pan of boiling water; bake at 350° for one hour or until a knife comes out reasonably clean.

Let stand on rack for 1 hour before unmolding. Cover with Topping. Serves many.

> Favorite recipe of Dorothy Rellas, author of novel, *Hidden Motives*, "Round Midnight" in the SinC/LA anthology, *A Deadly Dozen* and short story for *Futures* Magazine, "Let's Get to the Skinny." Board of Directors and treasurer 1997-2002.

"Blink once and you're dead."
"Blink twice and you're buried."—Chester Himes

POTENT POISON PUMPKIN PUDDING

3 cups canned pumpkin puree
¼ cup honey or 1½ cups sugar
2 tbsp. molasses
¼ tsp. powdered cloves
3 tsp. cinnamon
½ tsp. ginger
1 tsp. salt
4 eggs lightly beaten or egg beaters equivalent
2 cups skim milk, scalded (or 1can evaporated milk)

This low fat dessert is surprisingly rich and flavorful, a favorite Thanksgiving dessert. Preheat oven to 450°. Combine in one bowl the pumpkin, honey, molasses, cloves, cinnamon, ginger, salt, and eggs or egg substitute. On the stove, heat milk until a slight skin forms (scalded milk). Pour the milk into the rest of the mixture and combine. Butter a large enough casserole or baking dish. The pudding will rise an inch or two when it cooks. Pour the pudding into the baking dish and cook at 450° for 10 minutes. Reduce heat to 350° and cook for an additional 40 minutes or until the pudding is set (that's when the middle doesn't jiggle like a liquid).

Best served warm. You can add a dollop of whipped cream. Just like pumpkin pie without the crust.

Favorite recipe of Jamie Wallace, contributing author, "Driven to Kill" in the SinC/LA anthology, *A Deadly Dozen*, Board Member 1996-1997 and Vice President 1997-1999. Director for 1999 "No Crime Unpublished©" Conference.

"Justice is stupid. Death is blind."—Leonard Holton, *A Touch of Jonah*

"It is impossible ... not to make inferences; the mistake is to depend upon them ... In detention one should take no chances, give no one the benefit of the doubt."—Ronald Knox, *The Viaduct Murder*

"Riders, wriders, riters, writers, it's all the same to a poor speller."—DJB

PSYCHO PERSIMMON PUDDING
Or a bunch of loose nuts in a mess

1½ cups flour
1½ tsp. soda
½ tsp. salt
½ tsp. cinnamon
2 eggs
1¼ cups sugar
1½ cups sieved persimmon pulp
¼ cups melted butter or margarine milk
1 cup seedless raisins
½ cup chopped almonds
Purchased Hard Sauce or 1 cup whipped cream

Resift flour with soda, salt, cinnamon and set aside. Beat eggs until light. Beat in sugar. Stir in persimmon and melted butter. Add flour mixture alternately with milk, and beat smooth. Fold in raisins and almonds. Pour batter into a well-greased 9-inch loaf pan and set in a pan of hot water. Bake at 325° degrees 1-1½ hours, or until done. Serve warm with a dollop of hard sauce or whipped cream.

Favorite recipe of Alfred Hitchcock, director of *Vertigo, Psycho, To Catch A Thief,* and many more.

"People in glass houses—make good targets."—GTK

"It's elementary, my dear Watson—this is a killer cookbook."—Sir Arthur Conan Doyle

"Money, money, money, the root of all joy."
—DJB

REASONABLE DOUBT BREAD PUDDING

4 cups stale cinnamon rolls, coffee cake or bread
3 cups milk, warmed
pinch salt
3 large eggs, separated
½ cup sugar
1 tsp. vanilla
½ tsp. nutmeg
½ cup raisins
¼ cup orange or lemon marmalade (optional)

Preheat oven to 350°. Grease a large baking dish.

Dice the stale bread into cubes. Cover with the warm milk. Add salt. Beat together the sugar, egg yolks, vanilla, and nutmeg. Stir in raisins and marmalade. Stir this mixture into the soaked bread. Beat the egg whites until stiff. Fold into the bread mixture. Pour the pudding into the baking dish. Place dish in a large pan. and add ½-inch hot water to the large pan. Bake 50 to 60 minutes until pudding is set.

Favorite recipe of Mae Woods, television producer of *When Danger Follows You Home*, screenwriter for *Tales from the Crypt*, editor of *Murder by Thirteen*, SinC/LA anthology, and a SinC/LA Board of Directors member.

Rigor Mortis

The source of the term "stiff " for a dead person:

Brought about by the coagulation of protein in the muscles, it begins in the jaw and eyelids 1-4 hours after death and gradually spreads to the rest of the body. Full rigor is achieved after about 12 hours. It lasts for 12 hours, then gradually disappears over another 12 hours. Once rigor mortis is gone, it cannot return.

Be careful to arrange your victim in a mortuary fashion, especially if you intend to dispose of the body.

A YUMMY WAY TO DIE CUSTARD
A slim version of *crème brulée*,
the perfect disguise for a pinch of cyanide
for the victim who won't cheat on her diet.

2 cups nonfat milk
2 tbsp. nonfat powdered milk
¾ cup egg substitute
1/3 cup sugar
1 tsp. vanilla
2 tbsp. sugar

Preheat oven to 325°. Blend together milk, powdered milk, egg substitute, sugar, and vanilla in a blender. Set custard mixture aside. Sprinkle the 2 tablespoons sugar in an 8-inch cake pan and heat over low heat until the sugar is melted and golden brown. Cool slightly. Pour custard in cake pan. Place in a larger pan filled with 1 inch of hot water. Bake 1 hour or until custard is set. Chill and unmold to serve.

Favorite recipe of Mary T. Johnson, long-time and faithful SinC/LA member.

"It has been observed, with some truth, that everyone loves a good murder."—Tennyson Jesse, *Murder and Its Motives.*

"He was dead, all right. He has been shot, poisoned, stabbed and strangled. Either somebody really had it in for him or four people killed him. Or else it was the cleverest suicide I'd ever heard of."—Richard S. Prather, *Take A Murder, Darling.*

IN FOR THE KILL TIRAMISU

6 ozs. espresso coffee, made very strong
3 tbsp. Marsala wine
48 ladyfingers
4 large egg yolks or equivalent egg substitute
1½ cups superfine sugar (or use regular sugar, pulverized in the blender)
2 cups Mascarpone cheese
1 cup Ricotta cheese
1 cup heavy whipping cream
3 tbsp. unsweetened cocoa powder (Dutch process)

Mix the coffee with 1 tablespoon Marsala wine, then brush the mixture evenly over all the ladyfingers. Set aside. Beat egg yolks, slowly adding 1 cup sugar, until the mixture is smooth. Add the Mascarpone and Ricotta cheeses, blending well. Blend in ¼ cup sugar and the remaining 2 tablespoons Marsala wine. Set aside. Whip cream until stiff. Fold in remaining ¼ cup sugar, mixing well. Set aside.

Place 24 ladyfingers in the bottom of a rectangular glass dish. Spread with half of the egg yolk/cheese mixture, then half the whipping cream. Repeat the layers in the same order with the remaining mixtures. Dust the top with cocoa powder. Refrigerate at least 6 hours or overnight, before serving.

Favorite recipe of Susan M. Stephenson, author of "How to Grow Orchids Outdoors in Southern California," in the *American Orchid Society Bulletin,* and other articles about orchids, and public relations materials; Board of Directors, 1995–2002 as secretary, membership chair; *Ransome Notes* editor; and *Murder by Thirteen* anthology committee member and PBS Pledge Drive Coordinator.

The Usual Suspects

"In a homicide investigation we look first to gangbangers or thrill-seekers, those who think killing people is fun, because they love the high of the adrenaline rush. They're addicted to it. Then we look to the husband."—Quote from a twenty-five-year veteran homicide detective from a large southern California police department.

"Nobody is going to go to that much trouble to get murdered. But if you are going to murder somebody, you expect to go to a lot of trouble. I would."—Frances and Richard Lockridge, (film) *The Norths Meet Trouble.*

TERROR-MISU

¾ cup powdered sugar
2 cups whipping cream
8 ozs. Mascarpone cheese
8 to 10-inch Angel Food cake
¼ cup strong black coffee (espresso-like)
¼ cup + 5 tbsp. Kahlua or coffee-flavored liquer, divided
cocoa powder or grated chocolate

Whip the cream with ¼ cup powdered sugar and 2 tablespoons Kahlua, until stiff peaks form. Set aside. Whip Mascarpone cheese with ½ cup powdered sugar and 3 tablespoons Kahlua, until smooth. Fold ½ cup whipped cream mixture into the Mascarpone cheese mixture.

With a serrated knife, cut angel food cake into three layers. Prick lots of holes into all three layers. In a small bowl, combine coffee with ¼ cup Kahlua. Place the bottom layer of the cake on a plate or in a soufflé dish. Drizzle coffee/Kahlua mixture over the layer. Spread with half of Mascarpone mixture. Place second layer on top of first. Drizzle with coffee/Kahlua mixture and spread with remaining Mascarpone mixture. Top with cake layer. Frost top with remaining whipped cream mixture and dust lightly with cocoa or grated chocolate. Chill for up to 2 hours before serving. May be made the day before and served chilled. Keep refrigerated.

Favorite recipe of Kathleen Beaver, member of the SinC/LA Board of Directors, and Director of the 1999 "No Crime Unpublished©" Conference.

"He did not wear his scarlet coat,
    For blood and wine are red,
And blood and wine were on his hands
    When they found him with the dead,
The poor dead women whom he loved,
    And murdered in her bed ...

But each man kills the thing he loves,
    By each let this be heard,
Some say it with a bitter look,
    Some with a flattering word,
The coward does it with a kiss,
    The brave man with a sword!"

—Oscar Wilde from *The Ballad of Reading Gaol*

BLOOD DROP POPCORN BALLS

Pass these out at Halloween or your next mystery party to provide a little sweet horror.

2 cups sugar
½ tsp. salt
1 cup light corn syrup
1 cup water
1 tsp. vinegar
3 tbsp. butter or margarine
5 quarts popped corn
1 large bag red licorice pieces
Oil, to grease fingers

Combine sugar, salt, corn syrup, water, vinegar, and butter. Cook over low heat to the hard ball state (250° on a candy thermometer). In a large oven-proof bowl, combine popped corn with licorice pieces. Pour hot syrup slowly over popcorn and licorice. Mix carefully to coat all pieces. Grease your fingers and shape mixture into balls. Cool and wrap in red cellophane if desired.

Favorite recipe of Judith K. Smith, contributing author to SinC/LA anthology, *Murder by Thirteen*, past member Board of Directors. "No Crime Unpublished©" Conference Director; and is currently writing a Bea Silver mystery.

"Rule number something or other—never tell anybody anything unless you're going to get something better in return."—Sara Paretsky, *Deadlock*

"Never argue with someone bigger than you—unless you have the gun"—GTK

"Always look for the silver lining—or at least the silver."—GTK

CHOCOLATE SUPER SIN PASTRY
Sin today for tomorrow you die ...

1 sheet puff pastry, frozen
8 oz. semi-sweet chocolate chips
1/3 cup walnuts, chopped
1 tbsp. butter
Powdered sugar

Preheat oven to 425°.

Thaw pastry for 20 minutes, then roll out on a floured board to a 12-14-inch square. Place chocolate chips, walnuts, and butter in the center. Pull pastry edges together, twist, and put on an ungreased cookie sheet. Bake 20 minutes. Let stand 10 minutes, then sprinkle with powdered sugar.

Favorite recipe of Mary T. Johnson, a long-time and faithful member of SinC/LA.

Death By Freezing

Freezing to death does not, as a rule, produce any distinguishable injuries or changes in the body. At the autopsy, red spots may possibly be observed on those parts of the body where livid stains occur more rarely (e.g., the nose, tips of ears, fingers, and toes.). In most cases only the weak, helpless, insufficiently clothed or drunken persons are frozen to death. Quote from *Techniques of Crime Scene Investigations*, 6th edition, by Barry A.J. Fisher, Director, Scientific Services Bureau, Los Angeles County Sheriff's Dept.

Cold As the Grave Bittersweet Chocolate Ice Cream

¾ cup sugar
4 egg yolks (from extra large eggs)
1 cup heavy cream
1 cup milk
¾ cup buttermilk
7-oz. Scharffen-Berger chocolate (try to find this incredible gourmet cooking chocolate at http://www.scharffenberger.com)

Cream sugar and the eggs yolks in a bowl using a mixer until light and thick. Pour cream and milk into another large microwave-safe bowl, and cook at high power for 2 minutes.

Then keeping the mixer on, slowly pour the heated cream/milk mixture into the egg yolks. Mix until smooth and pour it all back into the microwave-safe bowl and put it back into microwave for 3 minutes, stopping every minute to whisk it. When it's thick enough to coat a spoon, add chocolate that's been broken into small pieces and whisk until chocolate melts.

Next, whisk in buttermilk (which enhances the chocolate flavor). Allow bowl to cool to room temperature and then place in the refrigerator (covered) for 3 hours, or overnight. Then pour into ice cream maker and follow maker's directions. Makes 1 quart.

For an amazing sundae, try drizzling with dark and white chocolate sauce and topping with fresh raspberries.

> Favorite recipe of Jerrilyn Farmer, author of *Sympathy for the Devil, Immaculate Reception* (nominated for a Lefty Award) and *Killer Wedding. Sympathy for the Devil* won the Macavity Award for the First Best Novel and was nominated for an Agatha, and an Anthony Award.

"Pride of any kind is a high place and any fall can kill."—John D. MacDonald, *The Girl in the Plain Brown Wrapper*

"Don't think I can't smell a cover-up."—Ferqus Hume, *Angel Eyes*.

"Intelligence has one moral law—it is justified by results."—John Le Carré, *The Spy Who Came in From the Cold*

CREEPY CAPER CREPES
Crepes vary as much as alibis do.

1½ cups flour
2 tbsp. sugar (a little more if you want it sweeter)
3 beaten eggs
1½ cups homogenized milk
2 tbsp. melted butter (no subs)

Whisk ingredients together except butter. Then slowly add the melted butter.

Optional: food coloring for festive holidays, extracts, herbs, grated orange, lemon, or lime peel. Make up batter 2-3 hours before using.

In a non-stick pan or crepe pan wipe with oil or butter after cooking each crepe. Cover the bottom of pan thinly and evenly with batter. When the crepe looks dry on top, it's ready to slip onto a wax-paper-lined dish. Use a paper between each layer. Repeat until all batter is cooked. Makes about 24 crepes.

They can be refrigerated for several days or frozen. Crepes must be completely defrosted to room temperature before rolling with filling.

Possible fillings:
Desserts:
Minced dates and chopped pecans drizzled with melted chocolate chips in a zigzag pattern; minced fresh fruit; jams and jellies.

Luncheons:
Stuff with cottage cheese and fresh fruit, chicken/turkey ala king, assorted steamed vegetables, Waldorf salad, or assorted cheeses and vegetables.

Favorite recipe of Diane Jay Bouchard, author of nonfiction magazine and newspaper articles and editor of *Desserticide II aka Just Desserts and Deathly Advice*. SinC/LA Board of Directors Vice President 1995-1997, and President 1997-2002.

Autopsy

During an autopsy, the victim speaks eleoquently to the coroner and is consider *the* silent witness—DJB

"Murder, though it have no tongue, will speak with most miraculous organ."—Shakespeare: *Hamlet*, Act II Scene 2

"Other sins only speak; murder shrieks out."—John Webster: *Duchess of Malfi*, Act IV

DONE IN BY ENGLISH TARTS
The Richmond Maids of Honor show their true wickedness with these fatally addictive mini tarts.

Pastry crusts (make, or buy two crusts)
¼ tsp. salt
½ cup sugar
3 tbsp. butter or margarine, softened
2/3 cup ground almonds
¼ tsp. almond extract
1 slightly beaten egg
4½ tsp. Raspberry jam

Roll pastry crusts to 1/8 inch thickness, and cut 18 circles, using 2½-inch cookie cutter. Fit circles into 1 inch deep muffin cups. Place ¼ tsp. jam in each uncooked shell (No more, or jam will burn).

Beat together the sugar and butter, or margarine, until creamy. Stir in almonds, almond extract, and egg. Spoon 2 tablespoons of the almond mixture on top of jam in pastry shells. Bake at 375° for 28 to 30 minutes or until golden brown. Remove from pan, cool on wire rack.

Favorite recipe of Esta Sullivan, former technical writer; member of SinC/LA nominating committee, 1999; and has just finished writing a novel.

"The trouble was a complex as good as Chardonnay, as hidden as the roots of the silent vines, and as deadly as the steel sliding between living ribs."—A.E. Maxwell, *Gatsby's Vineyard*

"Nothing is simpler than to kill a man; the difficulties arise in attempting to avoid the consequences."—Nero Wolfe, *Too Many Cooks*

The Elderberry Death Dance

In the 1970s, I lived in the Pacific northwest near neighbors who had a large fruit orchard. Elder devoured fruit pies, jams and jellies that his beloved wife, Millie, cooked or canned for him. One day she took raw elderberries and substituted them for kiwi in a cold soup recipe. Elder ate it and dropped dead.

If you want to dance with death these are the recommended ingredients: 6 pureed kiwis or equivalent volume fruit like watermelon, with mint leaves, 2 cups of plain yogurt, ¾ cup heavy cream, 3 tbsp. cider vinegar, 1 cup sugar, and ¾ cup apricot nectar blended until smooth. In another bowl, whip 1 cup heavy cream to soft peaks, beating in ¼ cup sugar. Fold into the mixture and chill. Serve in parfait or champagne glasses.

The moral of this recipe: Cooked elderberries are delicious. The raw elders killed Elder.

Favorite recipe of Joyce Spizer, author *of The Cop Was White as Snow* and *I'm Okay, You're Dead*, and non-fiction *Power Marketing of Your Novel.* Joyce is a licensed and legendary private investigator.

RED, BLACK AND BLUE BERRY TART

1 9" pastry tart shell
½ cup-2/3 cup purchased custard cream or small package vanilla pudding, cooked
1 cup blueberries
1 cup blackberries
1 cup raspberries
6 figs, halved lengthwise
1/3 cup red currant jelly
1 tsp. fresh lemon juice

Bake pastry shell according to directions; let cool completely before filling. Spread a thin layer of pastry cream over the bottom of cooled tart shell. Place the berries atop the cream, being as fancy or as casual as you wish with the arrangement. In a small pan, combine currant jelly and lemon juice and bring to a boil, stirring frequently. Let cool for a moment, then brush it on the fruit. Serve tart as soon as possible after assembling.

Favorite recipe of Marquis de Sade, author of novels, plays and short stories, and noted to be a bruiser of a human being.

Rigor Mortis Pecan Tarts

½ cup butter (no substitutes)
1 3-oz. package cream cheese
1 cup all-purpose flour
1 beaten egg
¾ cup packed brown sugar
1 tbsp. butter (no substitutes), melted
1 tsp. vanilla
½ tsp. almond extract
1 cup chopped pecans

Beat the butter and cream cheese in a small mixing bowl with an electric mixer on medium for 30 seconds. Stir in the flour. Cover and chill about 1 hour or until dough is easy to handle.

Form chilled dough into a ball. Divide dough into 24 equal portions; roll each portion into a ball. Place each ball into an ungreased 1¾ -inch muffin cup. Press dough evenly against the bottom and the sides of cup. Cover and set aside.

Filling: stir together egg, brown sugar, melted butter, vanilla, almond extract, and pecans in a small mixing bowl. Fill each dough-lined muffin cup with a scant tablespoon of filling.

Bake at 375° for 15-18 minutes or until filling is set and crust is lightly browned. Cool slightly in pans. Remove from pans and cool on wire racks. Makes 24.

Favorite recipe of coroners the world over.

SHERLOCK'S BANBURY TART

1 9" tart shell
1½ cup raisins
1 cup water
2/3 cup sugar
4 soda crackers, finely crushed
2 tsp. lemon zest, freshly grated
2 tbsp. fresh lemon juice
Egg, beaten

Preheat oven to 400°. Roll out pastry and line a 9-inch round or square tart pan. Bake partially, until pastry looks dry but still very pale. Cool completely before filling.

Topping:
½ cup all-purpose flour
3 tbsp. unsalted butter
2 tbsp. sugar
¼ tsp. salt

In a heavy bottom saucepan, combine raisins, water, sugar, crackers and lemon zest. Bring to a boil over high heat. Reduce the heat to low and simmer until slightly thickened, about 10 minutes. Remove from heat and stir in lemon juice and egg; set aside.

To make topping, combine flour, butter, sugar and salt in a small bowl. With your fingertips, blend together the ingredients until the mixture resembles fine crumbs.

Pour raisin mixture into a cooled tart shell and sprinkle the crumb mixture evenly over the top. Bake until lightly browned on top, about 35 minutes.

Favorite recipe of John Shannon, author of *The Concrete River* mystery series: *The Cracked Earth, The Poison Sky, The Orange Curtin* and *Streets of Fire.* Non-mysteries: *The Orphan, Courage, Broken Codes* and *The Taking of the Waters.* SinC/LA Board of Directors 2000-2002.

Colors for Writers (and Would-be Murderers)

As food is colorful, we offer the following advice to writers to use advantageously, and to murderers to use freely, or withhold as the case may be, on their would-be victims. *Warning:* Don't get the advice mixed up! Dire happenings could result!

Red: For writers: Stimulates and gives energy, strength, love, joy, enthusiasm, and a sense of adventure; releases adrenaline into blood stream and increases hemoglobin in blood.

For murderers: Lack of red leads to blood problems, weak vitality, anemia, bad circulation, worry, depression and fear.

Orange: For writers: Use when cold or depressed as it cultivates optiminism, self-confidence and the will to succeed.

For murderers: Lack leads to speen and kidney disorders, chest conditions such as asthma, hay fever and bronchitis.

Yellow: For writers: Stimulates brain, so keep nearby when you need ideas.

For murderers: Too much yellow causes nausea and may lead to constipation, diarrhea, indigestion, diabetes, liver eczema and skin problems.

Green: For writers: Provides natural balance and harmony, gives peace and tranquility and sedates nerves, and is one of the best colors for overall healing.

For murderers: Lack of green leads to cardiac problems, high and low blood pressure, neuralgia (head cold and pains), influenza, ulcers and cancer.

(Continued on page 156)

TNT Apricot Tarts

2 cups all-purpose flour
¼ cup sugar
¾ cup butter
1 egg
2 tbsp. cold water

Sift flour and sugar together; cut butter in finely. Beat egg; add cold water. Sprinkle lightly over the flour mixture; blend with a fork. Chill; roll thin. Line deep tart tins or medium muffin tins with pastry.

Filling:
1 egg
¼ cup corn syrup
¼ tsp. salt
1 cup brown sugar
¼ cup soft butter
12 large fresh apricots, ripened

Beat all ingredients except apricots thoroughly together. Halve the apricots; crack the stones from the center. Place one stone in each tart; cover with 1 tbsp. of filling. Cover with an inverted half apricot; add another spoonful of filling, using enough to fill the tarts two-thirds full. Bake at 375° until golden brown, about 25-30 minutes. Yields: 12 servings.

Favorite recipe of Nathan Walpow, author of *The Cactus Club Killings*, and *Death of an Orchid Lover*.

Colors for Writers (and Would-be Murderers)

Blue: For writers: Helps with clairvoyance and spiritual uplifting, raises consciousness, mental stimulation of truth, peace, poise, sincerity, and is the color of love; cultivates inspiration.

For murderers: Leads to sore throats, gum boils, teething, hoarseness, mouth ulcers, fevers and insomnia.

Indigo: For writers: Provides intuition; extends inner vision and opens one to new fields of knowledge; dispels negative thoughts and replaces them in the brain with positive thinking; removes fears; brings tranquility and a sense of at-one-ment.

For murderers: Leads to diseases of eyes, nose, ears, mental problems (obsession, insanity, nervous breakdown, alcoholic delusions), cataracts, facial paralysis and diseases of the lungs.

Violet: For writers: Color of spiritual knowledge and understanding; increases confidence; inspires mind; arouses awareness; brings self-esteem, inspiration and achievement.

For murderers: Color associated with power! Lack of violet leads to nervous and mental disorders, schizophrenia, sciatica, neuralgic headaches, concussion, infection, parasites, epilepsy, rheumatism, tumors, kidney and bladder weaknesses, leg and foot cramps.

Adapted by Gay Toltl Kinman from RWA Kiss of Death Chapter's online Murderone class taught by Mary Ogara.

TORCHED CRÈME BRULÉE

Sinfully rich without any way to torch the calories.

3 cups light whipping cream
6 egg yolks
1 tbsp. sugar
1½ tbsps. vanilla
¼ cup brown sugar, sifted

Put the cream in the top of a double-boiler. Carefully stir the egg yolks, beaten with sugar and vanilla extract, into the warm cream. Continue cooking gently until cream has thickened enough to coat the back of a wooden spoon.

Strain the cream through a fine sieve into a large soufflé dish or 6 small molds and chill for *at least 4 hours.*

Sprinkle a ¼ inch layer of sifted brown sugar over the chilled cream. Set the molds on a bed of ice cubes on the boiler pan and place under a hot broiler until the sugar caramelizes, *or* use a small kitchen propane torch to caramelize the top without using the broiler. Let the mixture cool then *chill in the refrigerator for 2-3 hours.*

Favorite recipe of Glynn Marsh Alam, author of *Dive Deep and Deadly*, a Luanne Forgarty Mystery; and has had short stories published by *Thema* magazine, Back Porch, Lonzie's Fried Chicken, *Illuminations* magazine and in the SinC/LA anthology, *Murder by Thirteen.* Glynn has won writing awards at the Southwest Writer's Conference, the California Writer's Conference and the Philadelphia Writer's Conference.

Digitalis

A useful poison that brings about death by heart failure and thus looks like the victim has suffered an unfortunate heart attack.

Digitalis is extracted from the leaves of the foxglove plant (*Digitalis purpurea*) and was used for many years in very small doses to regulate heart rhythms. In larger doses it is fatal within two or three hours.

UNDERCOVER PEAR PANDOWDY
Favorite of spooks, spies and private eyes.

1 cup firmly packed brown sugar
½ cup butter/margarine, softened
2 tbsps. all-purpose flour
¼ tsp. cinnamon
2 tbsps. lemon juice
5 cups (or 5 med-sized) peeled, cored, sliced 1/8" pears
   (apples may be substituted--rendering the recipe
   really "undercover")

Biscuits:
1½ cups buttermilk baking mix
½ cup milk
1 tbsp. sugar
¼ tsp. cinnamon
Vanilla ice cream, or whipped cream
   Heat oven to 400°. Combine brown sugar, butter, flour, cinnamon and lemon juice in a large mixing bowl.
   Beat at medium speed, scraping bowl often, until mixed well (1-2 minutes). Add pears; toss to coat. Spoon into a 2-qt. casserole dish. Cover; bake for 25-35 minutes or until pears are crisply tender. Meanwhile, combine baking mix and milk in a small bowl; stir until just moistened. Drop dough by spoonful onto hot pear mixture to make 9 biscuits. Stir together sugar and cinnamon. Sprinkle sugar mixture over biscuits. Return to oven, uncovered; continue baking 15-20 minutes, or until biscuits are lightly browned. Serve with ice cream or whipped cream.

Favorite recipe of Joyce Spizer, author *of The Cop Was White as Snow* and *I'm Okay, You're Dead*, and non-fiction *Power Marketing of Your Novel*. Joyce is a licensed and legendary private investigator.

Villainous Mango Freeze

4 cups peeled ripe mango, cut into 1-inch pieces (about 4
　　large mangoes)
¾ cup powdered sugar
½ cup mashed ripe banana
1 tbsp. fresh lime juice
1 8-oz. carton low-fat vanilla yogurt

Place mango pieces on a baking sheet lined with plastic
wrap; freeze for at least 4 hours. Remove from freezer; let
stand 10 minutes.

Place mango pieces in a food processor or blender; process until smooth, scraping sides of bowl occasionally. Add
sugar, banana and lime juice. With food processor on,
slowly spoon yogurt through food chute; process until
smooth, scraping sides of bowl once. Spoon mixture into a
freezer-safe container; cover and freeze 3 hours or until
firm. Note: let Mango Freeze soften a little before serving.
About 10 servings.

I'm sure that after a particularly grueling day of fending
off the advances of handsome middle-aged women in slit
shirts, and dusting his knuckles upside some ruffian's head,
PI Ivan Monk would settle down after a dinner he cooked
for himself and his significant other, Superior Court Judge
Jill Kodama, to a Villainous Mango Freeze. Followed, of
course, by a tumbler of whiskey and a Hoyo de Monterey
cigar on the backyard patio, while he listened to Miles Davis'
"Sketches of Spain" album on the stereo.

Favorite recipe of Gary Phillips, author of
Jook, and the Ivan Monk series: *Violent Sprint,*
Perdition USA, Bad Night is Falling and *Only*
the Wicked. PI Monk has appeared in sev-

eral short stories, including "The Sleeping Detective" in the Shamus Game anthology, edited by Robert J. Randisi. Gary has won the Brody Arts Fund Award for a radio script and the Co-founders Award from the Liberty Hill for political activism.

Antimony (Tarter Emetic)

Known since ancient times, antimony was used in cosmetics in Egypt and by medieval monks to reduce appetite while fasting.

Colorless and almost tasteless, antimony was the poison of choice in several famous Victorian murder cases, as its effects conveniently mimicked gastroenterites. Medicinally, it was used to induce vomiting, so care had to be taken by a poisoner not to overdose the victim, as the antimony would be expelled before it could kill.

Positive Self-Preservation

If you are a suspect in a crime, it is important to present yourself in a positive light to any police officers you encounter.

Think of the situation as a job interview where you want to make the most favorable impression possible. You will be viewed as a package of spoken and nonspoken signals. Be sure that what you say and how you act fit seamlessly together.

Maintain a high level of eye contact, lean forward, and keep an appropriate facial expression. Smiling should be avoided. Indications of subdued shock or distress can be effective. Be careful not to overact, as this may create suspicion, not lessen it.

WHODUNIT FRESH BLUEBERRY COBBLER
Not for the faint of heart

4 cups blueberries
1 tsp. lemon juice
Cooking spray
1 cup all-purpose flour
½ cup sugar
1 tsp. baking powder
1/8 tsp. ground nutmeg
Dash of salt
1 tbsp. vegetable oil
½ tsp. vanilla extract
2 egg whites, lightly beaten
3 tbsps. sugar
½ tsp. ground cinnamon

Preheat oven to 350°. Combine blueberries and lemon juice in a 9-inch square baking dish coated with cooking spray; stir gently, set aside.

Combine flour and the next four ingredients in a bowl; make a well in the center of the mixture. Combine oil, vanilla and egg whites; stir well with a whisk. Add it to the flour mixture, stirring just until moist. Drop dough by spoonful onto blueberry mixture to form 8 dumplings.

Combine 3 tbsps. sugar and cinnamon; sprinkle over the dumplings. Bake for 35 minutes or until filling is bubbly and dumplings are lightly browned. Serves 8.

Favorite recipe of Paula L. Woods, author of *Inner City Blues: A Charlotte Justice Novel*, which was named Best First Novel by the Los Angeles Times, the Black Caucus of the American Library Association, and has been nominated for an Edgar Award for First Best Novel.

INDEX

Author Recipe Contributors

Cakes

Candy

Cheesecakes

Coffeecakes & Bread

Cookies & Bars

Sauce

SinC/National

Special Acknowledgements

Tarts, Tortes & Other Sins

Tiramisu